David Galler is the son of ᵒᵘᵗˡⁱⁿᵉᵈ Jewish immigrants to New Zealand in the late 1940s and early 1950s, both now deceased. He lives in Auckland with his partner with whom he has two adult children.

For the past 25 years David has worked as an intensive care specialist at Middlemore Hospital. In 2011 he became a clinical director at Ko Awatea and chair of the Programme Committee of the annual APAC Forum. He has recently returned after a year working in Samoa. While there, he established an intensive care service to better identify and effectively manage infants, children and others with acute reversible disease and worked with the National Health Service and the National University of Samoa to establish in-country training for postgraduate medical education.

David was schooled at Wellington College. He gained his first degree from Victoria University in 1975 before becoming a bus driver with the Wellington City Council. In 1977 he was accepted to Otago University School of Medicine, graduating in 1981. Subsequently he went on to train in anaesthesia and then intensive care in London and New Zealand.

During his career, he has held a number of leadership positions, including Clinical Director of Acute Care Services Middlemore Hospital, Vice-president and President of the Association of Salaried Medical Specialists, Principal Medical Advisor to Ministers of Health and Director Generals of Health and was a foundation board member of the New Zealand Health Quality Safety Commission.

David Galler is the son of Anton Galler and Zosia Mine, Polish Jewish immigrants to New Zealand in the late 1940s and early 1950s, both now deceased. He lives in Auckland with his partner with whom he has two adult children.

For the past 25 years David has worked as an intensive care specialist at Middlemore Hospital. In 2011 he became a clinical director at Ko Awatea and chair of the Programme Committee of the annual APAC Forum. He has recently returned after a year working in Samoa. While there, he established an intensive care service to better identify and effectively manage infants, children and others with acute reversible disease and worked with the National Health Service and the National University of Samoa to establish in-country training for postgraduate medical education.

David was schooled at Wellington College. He gained his first degree from Victoria University in 1975 before becoming a bus driver with the Wellington City Council. In 1977 he was accepted to Otago University School of Medicine, graduating in 1981. Subsequently he went on to train in anaesthesia and then intensive care in London and New Zealand.

During his career, he has held a number of leadership positions, including Clinical Director of Acute Care Services Middlemore Hospital, Vice-president and President of the Association of Salaried Medical Specialists, Principal Medical Advisor to Ministers of Health and Director General of Health and was a foundation board member of the New Zealand Health Quality Safety Commission.

Things
That
Matter

Dr David Galler

Middlemore Intensive Care Unit

Things That Matter

Stories of
life & death

ALLEN&UNWIN
SYDNEY · MELBOURNE · AUCKLAND · LONDON

First published in 2016. This edition published 2017.

Allen & Unwin
Level 3, 228 Queen Street
Auckland 1010, New Zealand
Phone: (64 9) 377 3800
Email: info@allenandunwin.com
Web: www.allenandunwin.co.nz

83 Alexander Street
Crows Nest NSW 2065, Australia
Phone: (61 2) 8425 0100

A catalogue record for this book is available
from the National Library of New Zealand

ISBN 978 1 760631 53 6

Internal design by Kate Barraclough
Internal illustrations by Jo Pearson
Set in Sabon by Post Pre-press Group, Australia
Printed and bound in Australia by the SOS Print + Media Group

10 9 8 7 6 5 4 3

Contents

CHAPTER 1
The heart–
reliable, resilient, marvellous but sometimes the dumbest organ of them all   1

CHAPTER 2
Hat and hope is not a plan   27

CHAPTER 3
The kidney– ·
far too clever an organ to eat!   49

CHAPTER 4
The modern day plague–
weighing us down   71

CHAPTER 5
Medical revolutionaries–
we need more   93

CHAPTER 6
Close calls–
the thin line between life and death 121

CHAPTER 7
The ultimate gift–
life 143

CHAPTER 8
The art of medicine–
less is more 169

CHAPTER 9
My best ever patient–
72154 191

Acknowledgements 217
Glossary 219
References 225

To the memory of

Aron Galler
8 October 1912–2 May 1990

and

Zosia Galler
3 May 1929–8 June 2012

the heart

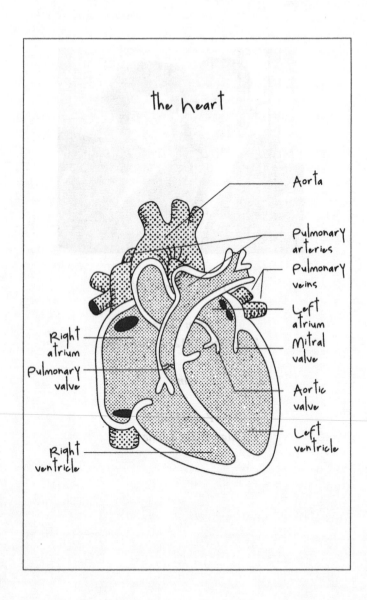

Aorta

Pulmonary arteries

Pulmonary veins

Left atrium

Mitral valve

Aortic valve

Left ventricle

Right atrium

Pulmonary valve

Right ventricle

The heart–

reliable, resilient, marvellous but sometimes the dumbest organ of them all

MY FATHER ARON GALLER died at 6 a.m. on 2 May 1990, the day before my mother's birthday. He was 77 years old. As he lay dying on the floor, his head in my mother's arms, he looked startled and asked, 'What's happening, Zosia?' Then he was gone.

Helpless, distraught and furious, my mother tried to bring him back to life by screaming and punching him. Needless to say it didn't work. His heart, the dumbest organ in the body, had stopped forever.

My mother called our GP, who came immediately. Too late to help Dad, she rang me as I was waking up to go to work at Middlemore Hospital in South Auckland.

I will never forget that phone call because of the guilt that welled up in me as soon as the phone rang. It was as though I already knew what had happened. You see Dad's death was not a surprise to me. We'd been talking on the phone a lot in the past few days and he had described to me what we in the game call crescendo angina—an escalation of chest pain that commonly leads to a heart attack and sometimes cardiac arrest.

My father was a good man. He came to New Zealand from Poland as a refugee in 1947. A lawyer by training he did what we Jews do well—he went into the schmutter business, in Dad's case, women's clothes.

When he first arrived in New Zealand he worked with his older brother Oser manufacturing women's coats, but after a near fatal fight they went their separate ways; Dad to the corner of Adelaide Rd overlooking the Basin Reserve. There he established a small manufacturing company and employed a dozen seamstresses, most of them, like him, refugees from Eastern Europe.

Dad had lived through interesting times, and he was kind and generous to a fault. He loved my mother more than anything and she depended on him for almost everything. Despite all of that his heart decided to stop and with that so too did the flow of blood and oxygen to all parts of him.

No, this was not a surprise. It was a consequence of many years of heart problems, which my brother and I jokingly blamed on my mother's cooking—especially her baked Polish cheesecake—and the second-hand smoke generated by her chain smoking. The cheesecake was a culinary IED; enough to give me angina just knowing it was on the kitchen table. Her other delight, the less poisonous Polish coffee cake, was simply too irresistible to leave alone and in the end must also carry some of the blame for my father's downfall.

My mother, Zosia Galler, was a socialite and the Polish coffee cake was baked fresh most days to feed the constant run of visitors to our house in the Wellington suburb of Wadestown. Mostly they were Eastern European friends of my parents who loved nothing more than a cigarette, a chat, coffee and cake. What was left over from the previous day's cake was eaten by my father. Every morning, elegantly attired in his silk dressing gown and hairnet, he could be found, knife in hand, dissecting out and eating the cake's rich veins of chocolate before demolishing the cake itself.

Dad's eldest brother, Oser, was married to Aunt Nina. She was also a heavy smoker—in her case not the mild Peter Stuyvesant or Rothmans that my mother loved but unfiltered Capstan Plain cigarettes. Oser had similar eating habits to those of my father. He loved picking from dishes in the fridge or on the stove but his penchant was for the savoury. He too died from heart disease. Maybe that will be my fate as well, but on average my family history suggests Zyklon B, the gas used by the Germans in the Second World War to exterminate so many Jews, as the most likely cause of my demise.

In my first year at med school in Dunedin, groups of us were assigned a cadaver. They were laid out on two rows of stainless steel tables that ran the length of a large, whitewashed, high-ceilinged room. Along both sides of the room were floor-to-ceiling windows, between them hung painted scrolls illustrating various parts of the human anatomy—the arterial system of the body with its blood full of oxygen, vessels coloured red; the veins of the body, its blood depleted of oxygen by the tissues of the body, coloured blue; the brachial plexus, nerves coloured yellow coming from the neck, going to the arm; the Circle of Willis, the beautifully designed arterial system at the base of the brain coloured red, and much more. In one such space was a floor-to-ceiling painting of the heart along with various drawings illustrating its chambers and valves, and one even showing the wiring system that accounted for the metronomic reliability that is its hallmark.

Nowhere was there a painting to illustrate what is commonly attributed to the heart: love, tenderness, and the range of emotions we all associate with it. Nowhere in the dissection of that organ did we see any hint of them either. It was an exercise that many in my group, still young and idealistic, found disappointing and sobering. Our heart was brown and rubbery, and smelled of formalin. Standing there in the dissection room, it was just another dead organ from the dead body in front of us. It was hard to believe that it could inspire such whimsy, let alone once have been that complex mix of flesh and blood; a pump, that slavishly served the brighter parts of us—our brain, liver and kidneys.

Although marvellous and reliable in some ways, the heart is the dumbest organ in the body—after all it keeps going in many people who might be better off dead, and stops in good people in the prime of their lives. It's an essential without which we are no more and, unlike our eyes and our kidneys, we have only one. There is no back up, no seagull engine for when the main motor fails, not even a set of oars. Because the health of our one and only heart is so imperative to our existence, modern society has made a massive investment to know everything there is to know about this essential bit of kit.

As a result of that, we now have expertise and technologies that are simply staggering. For the tiny baby born in Samoa with Tetralogy of Fallot—a complicated congenital abnormality of the heart that would lead to certain death if left untreated—treatments in first world health systems now exist.

Thanks to the skills of the local paediatricians, Makalita was diagnosed early and transferred to New Zealand where the four structural defects that make up the Tetralogy were repaired. That we can do that successfully in such a tiny baby will always amaze me.

As we move through the generations, there is a long list of other cardiac ailments any of us might be unlucky enough to acquire, each one of them countered by a range of increasingly effective treatments. As clever as we are though, the original design of our heart—G-d-given or refined over millions and millions of years—has proven to be impossible for us humans to match, even for those living with the gift of someone else's. This is sobering territory and a lesson for those looking for cures to their ailments, aches and pains in the deeds of men, because what's on offer from our best and brightest might not actually give you what you expect or want.

As an aside, the custom of substituting the word 'God' with G-d in English is based on the traditional practice in Jewish law of giving G-d's Hebrew name a high degree of respect and reverence. In short, this is a sign that the concept of G-d cannot be merely encapsulated in a word. Although I am not a religious man, for me, the substitution of the hyphen for a vowel adds a sense of mystery and awe.

When it comes to the heart, our best bet is to be both lucky and vigilant. Lucky that ours is a good one and stays that way, and vigilant to avoid the many threats to its ongoing well-being.

Recently, while on a ward round with the physicians at Moto'otua Hospital in Apia, I saw a young woman called Sepa. She was 24 and had not been so lucky. Sepa came from Savai'i, the big island, and had been admitted with severe heart failure and weight loss. Many years ago, as a child, Sepa—like so many others—had an infection caused by a particular bacterium called *Streptococcus pyogenes*, also known as the group A Streptococcus. The main symptom of these infections is a sore throat. Untreated or inadequately treated with antibiotics—simple penicillin is the antibiotic of choice—this can go on to cause an inflammatory condition that affects the valves of the heart.

Why this happens is the subject of much research. Each advance in knowledge throws up as many questions as answers, but what is clear is that this is a case of friendly fire. The bacterium has a protein in its cell wall that is similar to that on our heart valves. When our complicated and clever immune system kicks in to knock off the bacteria, those cells that are there to help us become confused and also attack the heart valves themselves. This low-grade assault can continue and intensify with further infections and exposure to the bacterium. Ultimately the inflammation that this causes can destroy the valves and ruin our hearts.

Once diagnosed, children who have suffered from a bout of acute rheumatic disease can still do well with regular injections of penicillin to halt or slow the progression of the disease. None of that happened with Sepa—watching her, miserable and uncomfortable on her bed, was heartbreaking and I knew then that she was not long for this world.

Under normal circumstances, the heart is a pump that circulates blood around the body. On the face of it, that might seem like a simple task but in reality it is more complex given the high degree of reliability we expect from this bit of muscle in the middle of our chest. Seventy-five beats a minute for every hour of every day of every year that we live. 4500 heart beats an hour; 108,000 heart beats a day, and over 1.5 million heartbeats a year for all of our lives. That is an awe-inspiring performance, especially considering that we are now living into our mid to late 80s.

The rhythmical comings and goings that make up each beat are also extraordinary. Set to music they are a symphony of coordinated intent that mere words cannot describe . . . but I will try anyway.

The heart is essentially a pump with two interdependent sides each with two chambers. The right pump and the left pump both work in parallel. Each side has an atrium into which blood first enters before being ejected into the main pumping chamber, the ventricle. Put simply, the right side of the heart circulates blood to and from the lungs, then the left side of the heart sends blood rich with oxygen to the tissues of the body. This flow of blood is so crucial to our well-being and is so cleverly designed it deserves a more detailed explanation: the heart receives 'blue' blood from the veins that drain the organs of the body once they have extracted the oxygen they need to continue to function. That venous blood enters the right side of the heart, initially into the right atrium—the upper right-hand chamber. Once there, following the coordinated contraction of the atrial muscles, the tricuspid valve between the right atrium and the right ventricle—the lower right-hand chamber—opens allowing the ventricle to fill. Then the muscles of the right ventricle begin to contract, closing the tricuspid valve behind it and eventually opening the pulmonary valve, ejecting blood forward into the pulmonary arteries. As the pressure in the right ventricle drops, it begins to refill and the pulmonary valve closes. From the pulmonary arteries, this 'blue' blood goes to the lungs where it picks up much needed oxygen and gets rid of the waste product carbon dioxide, which is ultimately expired by our lungs—another amazing bit of gear. This, the pulmonary circulation, is a relatively low-pressure affair in contrast with that performed by the left side of the heart.

The now oxygenated blood returns from the lungs to the left side of the heart, entering the left atrium. Once there the muscles of the atrium contract, opening the mitral valve and causing the blood to flow into the main pumping chamber of the heart—the left ventricle. As the muscles of the left ventricle contract, the pressure in the chamber rises to close the mitral valve and open the aortic valve ejecting blood rich with oxygen into the aorta at a high pressure, and from there to the tissues of the body.

As the pressure in the left ventricle falls the aortic valve closes, ensuring blood flows forward under pressure into the aorta and from there into the smaller arteries that carry oxygen to all of our organs and tissues. We call each beat from the left side of our heart our pulse and count its rate by the minute. We feel that in our wrists or arms or neck and sometimes when lying strangely we can hear it in our heads. The pressure that propels the blood is called blood pressure and we measure that with a cuff around the arm. These simple everyday terms barely scratch the surface of the complexity that underpins this marvellous servant that dances its dance with such coordination, reliability and grace. A video image of the heart at work set to music would be a certain Oscar winner.

In rheumatic disease, it is the left side of the heart that is mostly affected. For Sepa, her mitral and aortic valves were so damaged that as much blood was going backwards out of the heart as there was going forward in the direction it was supposed to go. As a result, her lungs were full of fluid and she was short of breath; her abdomen too was fluid filled and her liver congested. Her heart was so badly damaged that the only hope for her was transfer to New Zealand for surgery but by the time she came to us, it was too late even for that. Despite all efforts to help her, Sepa died three days after she was admitted to hospital.

Rheumatic fever is a disease that has largely been eradicated from much of the developed world but persists in populations that have a genetic predisposition to it accompanied by environmental factors like overcrowding and poverty. Māori and Pacific children seem particularly at risk, with an unacceptably high incidence of this disease in Samoa and in areas of New Zealand—like Northland, South Auckland, the East Cape and

Porirua—where there is overcrowding, economic deprivation and delayed access to health services.

My father died of ischaemic heart disease, a condition where the arteries that take blood and oxygen to the heart itself become increasingly narrowed. That disease first became evident when he was in his early fifties.

Dad was a good sleeper and, unlike me, had that ability to doze till late in the morning. Also unlike me, he was a private man, not one to share his worries or concerns. His heart problems became evident when he was 55—still a young man—when one morning, he was up uncharacteristically early and not wanting to wake my mother, he took himself to the kitchen, clutching his chest in pain. He was short of breath and he felt cold and clammy. Later he told me that he thought he was going to die. Unwilling to bother anyone he decided to ride it out sipping milk thinking it was a stomach upset. Thankfully my mother found him and called an ambulance.

Thinking this to be heart pain, the paramedics gave him oxygen to breathe, a spray of glyceryl trinitrate under his tongue and a small dose of morphine in the vein. Dad's pain immediately eased and he was taken to hospital. They were right, those paramedics. Dad's pain was classic angina pectoris; a shrill and alarming distress call by the cells of the heart when they become starved of oxygen. An electrocardiogram or ECG done at the time confirmed that. My father's pain was the result of a heart attack, which caused permanent damage to his heart. He spent a few days in hospital recovering then came home with a raft of medications as well as suggestions for an exercise programme, which he duly ignored.

Ischaemic heart disease contributes to the death of thousands of New Zealanders every year. Most at risk are those of us with a family history of the disease, being anyone with relatives who have suffered from the condition. Smoking, diabetes, high cholesterol, high blood pressure, poor diet, and a lack of exercise make our risk of disease and death even higher.

My father's reluctance to seek immediate help probably led to the irreversible damage done to his heart. But back then he was also lucky that his heart kept its rhythm because when it doesn't the consequences can be disastrous and sometimes fatal.

Every second week, for seven years, I commuted between my home in Auckland and work in Wellington. For my sins I was working half time as the Principal Medical Advisor both to the Minister of Health and to the Director General of Health. It was an interesting but exhausting time, and by the end of each week all I could think about was getting home.

One wintry Thursday afternoon, as I lined up to get on the 4 p.m. plane home, I happened to exchange glances with an affluent looking, middle-aged couple ahead of me in the queue. We briefly acknowledged each other in that polite way you do when you make eye contact with strangers. Once on the plane and underway on the hour-long flight, I stretched out as best I could and cast my mind forward to the weekend ahead. Suddenly the senior air steward walked past looking anxious then pulled an oxygen bottle from the locker above my head. 'Do you need any help?' I asked.

'Are you a doctor?' came her hopeful reply.

I got up and followed her down to row thirteen, to where that very same couple were seated. The well-dressed man in the aisle seat was slumped forward, his breathing noisy and his lips blue. He was unconscious.

I took the oxygen bottle from Sue, the air steward, and immediately put the mask on the man's face, pulling his jaw forward as I did. He pinked up fast. Even the passenger behind him noticed this, helpfully observing, 'His colour looks better.'

As I introduced myself to the man's partner, instinctively I felt for the pulse in his neck and was relieved to find that it was regular and strong. The couple, Maria and Don, were married and off to the States on a business trip. Maria told me that Don was 58 years old, in generally good health, and had no history of heart disease but took medication for high blood pressure. Quite suddenly, as she was telling me this, his pulse disappeared and Don stopped breathing.

In my language, we call this a cardiac arrest. A state where there is no forward flow of blood from the heart and no blood or oxygen being delivered to the tissues of the body. If not treated immediately people just die. If restoration of the person's circulation is delayed, the lack of oxygen to the tissues will cause varying degrees of damage to the body—especially to the brain.

I looked up at Sue and she looked at me. 'Cardiac arrest,' I whispered. She nodded towards the front of the plane.

With help from another passenger, we lifted Don out of his seat then carried and dragged him to the front of the plane, while at the same time ripping off his jacket and opening his shirt. Sue unpacked the on-board medical kit while I began giving him CPR (cardiopulmonary resuscitation) chest compressions at about 100 a minute.

The most likely cause of cardiac arrest in situations like this is a disorder of the heart's rhythm, called ventricular fibrillation (VF). When that happens all of the individual cardiac muscle fibres contract independently of each other instead of in the coordinated way necessary to eject blood out of the heart and into the tissues of the body. A heart in VF squirms and writhes rather than pumps and it looks as awful as are its consequences.

VF occurs in people with ischaemic heart disease and can be associated with a full-blown heart attack or with more minor bouts of ischaemia. Immediate restoration of the normal cardiac rhythm is possible by delivering an electric shock to the heart using a defibrillator.

'Is there a defibrillator in there?' I asked, while continuing the chest compressions. Every 20–30 compressions I briefly stopped to give Don an oxygen breath using an inflatable bag and a mask applied firmly to his face. Each time I did that his chest rose and I was pleased.

To my delight and relief, there was an automatic external defibrillator (AED) on board. It was yellow and called HeartStart—'Please,' I thought, 'yes please!'

These machines are cheap and clever. They are designed to be used by bystanders who have no training in resuscitation and they have saved thousands of lives worldwide. Cool and calm, Sue applied the pads to Don's chest, one on the chest wall just to the left of the midline below the throat, the other on the left side of the chest. The AED detects the patient's rhythm, tells you what it is and, if required, will automatically deliver the appropriate electric shock to the chest in the hope that it will restore the patient's normal heartbeat.

This HeartStart machine also had a small screen that displayed the patient's rhythm. As soon as we applied the pads it was obvious that the cause of this man's cardiac arrest was ventricular fibrillation. Crossing the screen was the telltale pattern of VF, an uneven, chaotic pattern of up and down lines. Before I could say, 'All clear!' and activate the electric shock, the machine announced in an American accent, 'Shockable rhythm. Shockable rhythm. All clear. All clear.'

Then boomph! 200 joules of energy shot down the wires into

the pads and via them through the patient's chest and across his squirming heart.

Lo and behold, after a very brief pause, across that little screen a more orderly picture emerged—something we call normal sinus rhythm. In his neck where there was once a pulse and then there wasn't, I could feel a pulse again. Slow at first and a bit weak because he was quite blue. However, with more regular oxygen breaths, Don became increasingly pink and his heart rate went from 30 beats a minute to 60 to 90 to 110. Although still deeply unconscious, I felt his own respirations begin to kick in again.

It was only then that I looked up for the first time. I was jammed into the window of the first row of the plane. The man's legs stretched across the aisle into the area where patients board. It seemed that the world had stopped because there was complete silence on board. You could have heard a pin drop and around me I saw the saucer-like eyes of other passengers staring at me.

Opposite me was the deputy prime minister, who I'd clashed with over health policy some years earlier, and I thought, 'Bugger you! Not bad for a "mere public servant", eh?' He looked away with no sign of acknowledgement, not even a smile or a wink.

Although it felt like an age, this had all taken less than five minutes. I put a drip in Don's arm and as we got closer to Auckland he began to rouse in an irritable and unhelpful way—a good sign I thought but potentially not so helpful right then so I gave him a small dose of sedation to keep him calm until we reached Auckland.

Once we landed, the passengers disembarked from the rear door and the paramedics came on board. We intubated Don, placing a breathing tube in his windpipe to take control of his breathing and to make him more secure for his ambulance ride to my second home, Middlemore Hospital.

He did well, that man. After a couple of days sedated and on a ventilator doing what we could to maximise the chances of a good neurological recovery, we stopped the drugs keeping him asleep—Propofol, and Fentanyl, a short-acting narcotic—so we could see what he was like.

He woke up pretty well. When we told him what had happened, he smiled a smile that I will never forget—big and wide, as if he knew instinctively how close he had come. He was momentarily dead, then alive again. What a weird stroke of luck. He recovered fully and resumed his life.

His wife bought me a shirt as a gift—it's gorgeous and every time I wear it I think of her and of him. It turns out I know his GP so I still get the occasional update on how he's doing—he's still working but now divorced! I was sad to hear that but I suppose it's hard to think you can be the same person after living through something like that.

He really was lucky because the outcome for patients who suffer an out-of-hospital cardiac arrest is always uncertain. For those whose collapse is due to VF, immediate defibrillation will deliver the best likelihood of a full recovery. Many who collapse and receive immediate and effective bystander CPR, followed by defibrillation and a quick restoration of their own cardiac rhythm, may also do well. However, the longer the delay between collapse and restoration of the heart's natural rhythm, the worse the person's outcome.

Don's life was saved by the immediate availability of a cheap, easy-to-use AED. In some parts of the world—Seattle is perhaps the best example—AEDs are everywhere and their locations are widely known. In the event of a collapse, emergency services will even direct bystanders to the nearest one. Do you know where your nearest one is? It would be a good idea to find out. If there isn't one near you, maybe you or your employer should buy one and ensure the people in your building know where it is kept. It might be that one day you or one of your mates might wake up with a smile on your face having joined the growing numbers of people who were gone but came back.

When poor outcomes result, they are due to damage to the brain—the one organ in the body whose tissues will not tolerate a cessation in oxygen delivery for more than a few minutes. Sadly, the parts of the brain that are most likely to be damaged first are the ones that make us uniquely who we are, those parts of the brain that have evolved most recently and set us apart from other forms of life, giving us the ability to socialise, remember, recognise, love and contribute.

Unlike my father, who had every reason to have a cardiac arrest, this appalling event can be visited on the young and seemingly well. Tiara was just such a person—a bright 20-year-old studying commerce at a university a long way from home.

Like many of her friends, she worked hard but she was social too. One Friday evening she was out with friends, bar hopping and dancing till the early morning. Although the story will always be a little vague, it seems that Tiara got home just after 2 a.m. and went straight to bed. About an hour later her flatmates heard a noise from her bedroom and went in to investigate. From what they later described, it seemed like Tiara was having a convulsion; she was thrashing about the bed unresponsive and frothing at the mouth. They called an ambulance and waited.

By the time help arrived Tiara had stopped breathing and she was blue. The two paramedics were young and efficient. It was immediately clear to them that Tiara didn't have a pulse so one of them began CPR. The other attached the defibrillator leads, which showed the flat line of asystole—no electrical rhythm at all—and then slipped a breathing tube into her wind-pipe to give her some oxygen. In between breaths, she also put an intravenous line (IV) into a vein in her arm and gave Tiara an immediate 2 milligram injection of adrenaline to help kick start her heart. All the while her colleague continued the chest compressions at about 100 per minute. This sequence of events I know so well—chest compressions, oxygen breaths and intra-venous adrenaline was repeated many times over the next twenty minutes.

Then quite suddenly Tiara's heart kicked back into action, all over the place at first but soon resuming its regularity like nothing had happened. She had a pulse and soon pinked up nicely, but she remained deeply unconscious on her way to hospital.

For some, like Tiara, who suffer a prolonged cardiac arrest, if we persist with resuscitation, the heart will often kick back into action oblivious of damage already done elsewhere. For healthcare providers, once a patient is resuscitated—no matter how long they may have been 'down'—it becomes a waiting game during which any obvious cause of the arrest is treated and damage control measures are put in place to give the brain the best chance of recovery.

Although the events surrounding a collapse and arrest might not seem to bode well for a good recovery—in this case, a prolonged down time and no bystander CPR before the return of a sponta-neous circulation—we have no technology or tools to accurately assess what the true outcome will be other than by waiting and seeing. That wait will usually be several days while the patient is kept in an induced coma. At the right time, often at 72 hours post-arrest, any drugs keeping them asleep are stopped and the patient is assessed. For distraught families desperate for a good outcome, this is a dreadful time full of fear, hope and prayers.

Tiara's cardiac arrest may well have been the result of a prolonged seizure and the lack of oxygen that can so often accompany that. Why she had the seizure we may never find out—she had never had any before and the tests that were done to identify potential causes, including a comprehensive toxicology screen looking for evidence of drug ingestion, proved negative.

The heart, our reliable servant in so many ways, is a resilient organ and can put up with a lack of oxygen much better than other tissues of the body, especially the brain. The one organ in the body that so defines us as who we are, the brain might tolerate a lack of oxygen for two to three minutes but if that persists for much longer, some damage and lasting effects will result. On the face of it then, Tiara's story was worrying. There had been a five-minute delay before the paramedics arrived and another twenty minutes of CPR before her own heart finally started.

The initial finding of asystole, the flat line on the monitor, was also a worry. If our theory was correct—that the cardiac arrest was the result of a prolonged seizure and with it a long period where her breathing was so badly affected her tissues were starved of oxygen—her brain would certainly have suffered significant damage well before her heart had stopped.

This proved to be the case. Once in hospital, Tiara was managed in the intensive care unit (ICU). She was kept sedated with Propofol and on a ventilator for the first few days, while medical staff concentrated on providing the treatments and care that would create the best chances for Tiara's brain to recover. Her temperature was controlled to keep her at 36.5 degrees Celsius; the head of her bed was elevated to 30 degrees; her blood pressure, the CO_2 and sodium levels in her blood were managed to minimise any swelling of her brain. Those treatments persisted for 72 hours, apart from short periods twice a day when the sedation was stopped to allow Tiara to 'wake up' so she could be assessed.

Propofol, the drug we give by intravenous infusion to keep intensive care patients either sedated or anaesthetised depending on the circumstances and dose, is a medication I now refer to as the 'Michael Jackson drug'. It is white and looks like milk. Sadly for Michael Jackson, in his case it was inappropriately prescribed, almost certainly not monitored, and seemingly implicated in his death. In our hands, Propofol is safe and extremely useful as a sedative agent. Its effect is short lived so once stopped, our patients will emerge 'clean' and not befuddled by other medicines enabling us to make an accurate clinical assessment of their level of consciousness.

That bedside assessment is beguilingly simple. It does not involve expensive technology or tests. It is based on clinical observation and the responses we get to simple stimuli. The best result we might expect to see from a patient emerging from sedation following a cardiac arrest is that they wake normally, open their eyes and respond appropriately to commands showing an understanding of what is asked of them: open your eyes, squeeze my hand, poke out your tongue are the kinds of things we commonly start with.

The worst result is when people don't wake at all, remaining deeply unconscious with their eyes closed and showing no response to voice or a painful physical stimulus. In between those two poles there exists a range of responses that have been correlated with outcome. Those responses form the basis of the Glasgow Coma Scale (GCS), first described by two Glaswegian neurosurgeons, Graham Teasdale and Bryan Jennett, to describe levels of consciousness associated with a traumatic brain injury. Their scale—from a normal score of 15 to the worst score of 3—is now part of everyday medicine and used to assess level of consciousness no matter the cause.

Twenty-four hours after her admission to the intensive care unit, ventilated and sedated still, Tiara looked good. Walking into her bed space there was a sense of calm and all was tidy. Her pupils were briskly reactive when I shined the bright light of a small torch into them. From the monitor above her head came the reassuring regular bleep associated with a steady pulse, and on its screen was displayed a normal heart rate, blood pressure and oxygen saturation. By this stage too, all Tiara's blood results had returned to their normal ranges. A clean sheet covered her from the neck down and her hair had been washed and neatly brushed. If it wasn't for the breathing tube in her mouth you might have thought she was just a pretty young woman having a sleep.

Her nurse, always at the bedside, stopped the Propofol infusion, which was running at 10 millilitres an hour, and we waited. Although Propofol wears off in a couple of minutes, it sometimes takes a little longer for a patient's underlying state to emerge. This first time, despite waiting for over half an hour, Tiara showed no spontaneous sign of wakefulness. The only change was that she had started to take some breaths for herself. Her eyes remained closed and she showed no response to the pain of me pressing down on her eyebrow, then applying pressure to the nail beds of her fingers and toes. She had the lowest recordable GCS, a score of 3, a real concern but perhaps not unexpected.

Tiara was the eldest of seven children. Her mother had died three years before and the rest of her siblings lived on the family farm with their dad and two aunties. By this stage, all the family had arrived at the hospital and were with me when we stopped the Propofol. We had already spoken, initially by phone then more formally several times as various family members arrived at the hospital. Despite those conversations and my obvious anxiety about how this would work out, they were a devout family and remained more optimistic than I was about a good outcome for Tiara.

Over the next few days we repeated the exercise of stopping the Propofol and allowing Tiara to wake. Each time there were some changes but none of them particularly hopeful for a good recovery. Her breathing would quicken and deepen and she would sweat. After a few days, her eyes would open to a painful stimulus, her pupils would rove from one side to the next and she would roll her shoulders inward then straighten and stiffen her arms and legs. I recognised these as signs of severe neurological damage, but her younger sister April thought Tiara recognised her and responded to her voice. I could see no sign of that—to me it was time to accelerate the difficult but essential conversation with the family about next steps.

I explained that, in time, it might become apparent that despite our best efforts not only would Tiara not improve, she would most likely deteriorate. Should that occur, our ongoing active support would hold no hope of bringing her back. If that were to happen, I asked whether they would agree with our plan to recognise the limitations of what we could achieve ourselves and turn our attention to Tiara's comfort. Our goal then was to return her to a more natural state or as I so often say to families, put her in the hands of G-d.

I spoke about the dishonesty of pretending to be able to do things we simply cannot do, and the indignity of prolonging suffering and hope when there is no hope to be had from our interventions. Allowing a family to believe that we can cure and fix things we clearly cannot is a lie. It does a great disservice to all of us and to the credibility of medicine as a whole. This was the nature of our discussions over the next ten days.

By this stage Tiara was breathing for herself and off the ventilator. She was being fed through a nasogastric tube that was passed through her nose, ran down the back of her throat, down her oesophagus and into her stomach. During this time, the family and I reached an agreement that we would not escalate care by putting her back on the ventilator should she deteriorate.

Although mostly deeply unconscious and not doing much, those episodes of 'physiological distress' became increasingly frequent. Perhaps triggered by hearing sounds or being stimulated by a touch, her breathing would again quicken and her pulse race; she would sweat profusely and her limbs would roll and stiffen. This was truly awful. There was no coming back from this—of that I was certain.

As those abnormal movements intensified, my conversation with the family turned again to her level of consciousness and whether she was aware of the distress so evident to us. At the same time, more and more of the family could see what I could see but a small group held on to the belief that she would improve, that G-d would save her with a miracle or that there would be a test or a procedure that would eventually make her better. Staunchest of those was her younger sister April, a university student like Tiara. She loved her sister dearly, and it was this love and her sense of devotion and duty to her to 'not give in' that was the barrier to her accepting the truth that nothing would restore Tiara to the happy, smart, fun-loving sister and best friend that she once was. Maybe I was a bit slow understanding this but once I did our conversation reached a new and much more meaningful level while reassuring and acknowledging April's love and devotion to her sister.

Soon we agreed a new goal for Tiara, not the impossible—pretending to be able to restore her to her former self—but to make our main priority the maintenance of her comfort and her dignity.

And so we began a low-dose infusion of medicines to make true what we had all agreed—a cocktail of morphine, haloperidol and hyoscine continuously and slowly delivered just under the skin on Tiara's belly. Within an hour a quiet peace settled over her and in the room. Overnight that sense of calm allowed the emergence of a new set of conversations about Tiara, about her childhood and the funny and silly things that were so much a part of her growing up. April, her devoted sister, laughed and cried. The eleven-year-old twins, once frightened and terrified, seemed to relax, looking on wide-eyed at the events that were unfolding around them. Their dad John, never the same person after the death of his wife, smiled too. Several days later, peacefully, quietly, free at last, Tiara drifted off.

The following day I met with the family for the final time. They too were at peace. Tiara's aunt Tia pulled me aside to thank me and to tell me—with a sense of relief and acceptance—that Tiara had passed on the ninth and final day of the novena. I smiled, having no idea of what she meant.

My father's death still lives with me, although with the passing of time I have forgiven myself for many of the things that for so long I beat myself up about.

How could I have not gone down to Wellington earlier? Perhaps I could have done more to help him? What could I have done? Suggested he go back into hospital?

Dad hated hospitals. During his last ever admission for chest pain ten years before he died, he became delirious and had terrible nightmares. He was aware of what was happening and felt deeply hurt and insulted by the way the staff had treated him. He signed himself out and never went back. In fact, he went directly to see the family lawyer, the expensive one whose signature ran across the entire width of an A4 page, to sign an advance directive stating that he would never go back to Wellington Hospital no matter the circumstances. My father was a hot-headed man at times.

If I had been there, could I have helped him at home? Was it fair that he died alone with my mother?

I know that if I had been there my mother would have wanted me to resuscitate him and I know that Dad would never have wanted that. If I was there and didn't try or tried and failed, I am not sure that in her heart, my mother would ever have been able to forgive me.

If I had been there at least I could have told Dad one last time how much I loved and admired him.

He knew that but this and many more things still play on my mind today.

'The end matters,' wrote Atul Gawande in his book *Being Mortal*, 'the end matters because that's what we remember and that's what we carry with us as we grow up and as we grow old.'

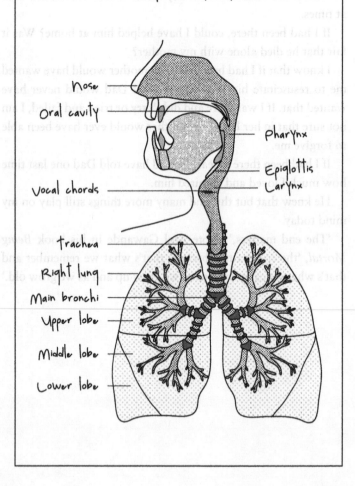

The Respiratory System

nose

Oral cavity

Pharynx

Epiglottis

Vocal chords

Larynx

Trachea

Right lung

Main bronchi

Upper lobe

Middle lobe

Lower lobe

Hat and hope is not a plan

I SURVIVED MY CHILDHOOD and adolescence, as did my brother. Many don't. That's not to say we didn't have close shaves. We both had our share of those but each time we were saved by circumstances rather than by luck, by a safety net many don't have.

My parents were Polish Jews, refugees to New Zealand who ate pork and made yoghurt out of sour milk. We lived in Wellington in a house always full of visitors with strange names. They were a mad and flamboyant lot.

My parents' love for me and my brother was never in doubt, so despite our close calls and near death experiences my brother and I remain full of forgiveness and understanding for their failings as parents. They were brought up in another time, a time so full of turmoil and grief that even simple everyday tasks like cooking had to be learned afresh.

There were no parenting lessons in Auschwitz so who can blame my mother for my brother's 'failure to thrive', a weight loss that continued for weeks after the new mum and her first-born returned home to their small house. Still struggling with the English language, my mother was unable to fully comprehend the instructions on how to mix his formula feed. Despite my brother's best efforts, the thick goo that filled the bottle could not be sucked through the bottle's teet. Poor Leslie, that combination of extreme exercise and underfeeding almost killed him, but he was saved at the last moment by the heroic Dr Harding, our GP—a patient man reliably attired in a three-piece suit and a hat. He came to our house for a morning and simply watched what my mother was doing and saw in an instant what the problem was.

My first brush with death happened a few years later when I was six weeks old. We lived in a little house in Palmer St near where the old Wellington Tennis Club once was. Mum was at home alone with me, Les was at a Catholic preschool—another close call—near the Basin Reserve and Dad was at work. It was winter and the house was cold. I was asleep in the front room when the curtains caught fire on the heater. Mum was at the back of the house in the kitchen. Luckily my father came home for lunch and saw the smoke. Yelling out, he rushed into the front bedroom, grabbed me from the cot and threw me out of the window onto the lawn, only to have my mother berate him because I might catch a cold. Say no more, now you have it.

At age six, Leslie was run over by a bus and ended up with a broken femur. He spent six weeks in Wellington Hospital, his leg in traction. In those days, hospitals were fearsome institutions run by strict but well-meaning people who knew best. Visiting, even to the children's ward, was restricted to two hours in the afternoon and two hours in the evening. This became intolerable for my mother, who used to climb the drainpipe to the first floor to get a glimpse of my brother and for my brother to see him. Dad hated that place from then until his dying day. How odd it is then that both his sons have spent all their working lives in hospitals like that one in Wellington; I would like to think on a 'mission from Dad' to humanise them.

When I came back from a long stint working abroad, I finished off my postgraduate training in Auckland at a time when Auckland's hospitals—Middlemore, Greenlane, Auckland and Princess Mary—were all part of the Auckland Area Health Board. That and the constant complaints about doctors' car parking were perhaps the only two things that they had in common because on all other fronts they were very different places with very different cultures.

The head of the regional anaesthetic service at the time was a distinguished man called Dr Watt. Tall, handsome and wise, with silver hair and a sharp parting, he saw immediately that I was a Middlemore man and happy to do G-d's work in South Auckland. I was no pointy-headed professor in platform heels that was for sure, so to Middlemore I went and to this day I remain grateful for his direction.

I say 'G-d's work' because of the immediately obvious and seemingly ever rising tidal wave of need in South Auckland, especially in the area of child health where the impacts of poor education, housing and low household incomes played out in such an egregious way.

A stark illustration of that was in the early to mid 1990s with the emergence of the epidemic of childhood disease caused by the bacterium *Neisseria meningitidis* serotype B, also known as meningococcus. This bug lives in the nasal passages of up to 15 per cent of us and can be spread by sneezing, coughing or sharing saliva. Although the causes of an epidemic are complicated and involve a change in many factors, it is widely accepted that the tipping point for this epidemic was the removal of the housing benefit in 1991. This forced families to live together in overcrowded houses, thereby increasing the risks of exposure to many more people. It was also clear that an individual child's chance of developing meningococcal disease was related to the number of adults living in the house.

Unsurprisingly, the highest infection rates were among Māori and Pacific Island children under five years of age, many of whom presented to Middlemore Hospital critically ill. The infection we called meningococcaemia described a systemic illness caused by this bacterium entering the blood stream that led to a rapidly progressive deterioration in organ function characterised by profound shock, respiratory failure, a depressed level of consciousness, and a tendency to bleed—initially causing a small pin-prick haemorrhage in the skin then the blotchy, blue, non-blanching bruise we call an ecchymosis. Children don't have the reserves of adults so when they become critically ill and stop eating and drinking, as did all of these infants, they can quite quickly develop dangerously low calcium and glucose levels, which on their own can be life threatening if not immediately treated.

The illness can be hard to pick at first and presents with symptoms similar to that of the common cold and flu—fever, headache, nausea, runny eyes, sore throat, runny nose, and cough. Some children with these general symptoms were seen by medical staff and sent home only to return with more advanced disease later. Tragically, a smaller number died at home.

During those early months of the epidemic, we were seeing up to four infants and children with advanced disease every day in our emergency department at Middlemore Hospital. Some died and many were left with serious disability as a result of the disease causing blockages to the circulation of blood in small blood vessels leading to the loss of digits and, in some cases, whole limbs.

We learned very quickly from those deaths, becoming super aggressive in our management of those kids. So too did the general community. As word of the epidemic spread, families became increasingly vigilant. They brought their sick kids to the doctor and our emergency department much earlier and for a wider range of symptoms. Family doctors stepped up giving these kids shots of penicillin with one hand while they called for an ambulance with the other.

The epidemic peaked in 2001 with 650 cases (17.4 cases per 100,000 people), and finally was put to bed with an immunisation campaign in the mid-2000s. In total 252 deaths were attributed to meningococcal disease between 1991 and 2007.

How ironic that such a destructive and nasty disease can be caused by a bug that is so sensitive to penicillin, our first antibiotic, discovered by Alexander Fleming in 1928. Even in the worst cases of disease, three days of intravenous treatment with penicillin will rid the body of the meningococcal bacteria. If only that was enough to halt the progression of this terrible disease!

We human beings are a complicated mix of biochemistry and biology—a dynamic boiling soup of molecules and biochemical reactions, some pulling us to the left, some pulling us to the right; others pull us up, some pull us down. When we are well, that push and pull seems to keep us uniquely balanced in the centre, a concept we call homeostasis—a term to describe the property of a system in which variables are regulated so that internal conditions remain stable and relatively constant.

Critical illness and injury play havoc with that fine balance. So despite access to antibiotics that kill the bacteria that causes disease, the consequences of the infection can continue to progress.

When I explain this to the families of my patients, I sometimes use another analogy—that of dominoes. Think about a line of dominoes and off each and every domino in that line is another line, and off every one of those is another line.

The initiating disease is like a boot kicking over a few of those dominoes. As they fall, so too do more and more dominoes around them. The rate at which that happens and the extent to which the dominoes continue to tumble is related to factors unique to that patient like their genetic makeup, the intensity and nature of the insult they have been subjected to, and the timeliness, effectiveness and accuracy of our treatments.

Despite removing the boot, or killing the bacteria with antibiotics, the consequences of the disease or injury can continue and for some are life threatening and for others, fatal.

Josh has just celebrated his twenty-first birthday. He is a lovely young man, quite sporty and now at the end of his university studies. On the face of it, he is just like many young people of a similar age—but Josh is different. On close inspection, you might notice that he has lost the tips of his fingers on both hands and, when he wears shorts, you can see his prosthetic leg—his own lost to meningococcal disease when he was a baby.

He became ill when he was only five months old. His mother remembers it like it was yesterday. At about 5 o'clock one afternoon, Josh developed a fever, quickly becoming sleepy and irritable. Thinking he was hungry, his mum tried to feed him but Josh was too drowsy to care. By the time he arrived in the emergency department he had a temperature of 40, was breathing fast and was already struggling to maintain normal oxygen levels in his blood, a condition we call hypoxia. His heart was racing, his circulation was poor and he had cold blue fingers. When we press on the finger tip of a well child the skin will blanch. When we release the pressure, it should take less than three seconds to pink up. This is called the capillary refill time and, in Josh's case, it took a sluggish six seconds.

It was obvious what the problem was. He, like so many before him, had meningococcal disease. The telltale petechial rash, at first sparse—just a few pinhead-sized, reddish-blue spots were present on his chest and abdomen. Although easy to miss at first, they became increasingly evident, and before our eyes some of his fingers and toes mottled and darkened.

It was 1997 and we were hitting our stride with this disease. We were over the soft and gentle approach to kids presenting like this—we'd already seen too many die. I took over the airway, giving him high-flow oxygen while another doctor slid a drip into a vein in his foot, taking bloods at the same time. His blood sugar was low so we topped him up with a push of 50 per cent dextrose, some calcium, 20 millilitres per kilogram body weight of fluid, and a big dose of antibiotic.

As we were doing all of that, we prepared to take over his breathing to allow us to treat him more aggressively. We gave him small doses of drugs to get him to sleep and to stop him moving. A breathing tube was then inserted through one of his nostrils into the back of his mouth, and on down between his vocal cords into his trachea. This was followed by a nasogastric tube which drained a ghastly black fluid from his stomach, almost certainly a collection of old blood and stomach acids that typically accumulate in very sick kids.

We put him on a ventilator and went to work giving him more fluid, inserting new lines and beginning infusions of drugs to improve his heart function and circulation.

Critical illnesses like this follow different phases before they resolve, one way or another. Initially, there is a dramatic spiralling down and progressive deterioration of organ function—a descent towards death that we chase hard to slow and stop by taking control of the patient's physiology, using aggressive fluid resuscitation, drugs to improve the circulation, ventilation and acute dialysis to restore a more normal milieu for the patient's organs to operate in. With luck that will be followed by a period of relative stability as we continue to support the various organs of the body with our machines and drugs in the hope that people will have the strength to regroup and get better and, with our help, fend off new assaults from infection and the complications of the various treatments.

Over the next few hours, we worked hard to keep up with the chaos that was Josh's physiology—more and more fluid, plasma and platelets to replace the clotting factors in his blood that were being consumed in forming the clots blocking the small vessels in his fingers, toes and other parts of his body; higher and higher doses of drugs to improve his circulation and the performance of his heart; more support on the ventilator.

As time passed, his descent slowed and he became a little more stable. By the next morning the worst was over, but he was left with black fingers and a dusky left leg from mid-shin down. That phenomenon, called *Purpura fulminans*, is the result of small vessels becoming blocked with debris that results classically from infection with this deadly bug *Neisseria meningitidis* and seen also with its equally deadly friend, the group A streptococcus.

Three days after his admission, Josh was discharged from ICU to the paediatric ward, and later went on to have a below-knee amputation of his left leg as well as losing the tips of a few fingers on both hands. Two weeks later, he was back at home.

Meningococcal disease still occurs but it is now more commonly due to the group C variant of the bug and it is adolescents who are most at risk. Because it too is spread by droplets through sneezing, coughing and sharing drink bottles, overcrowding or close living is again a factor. Typically we see outbreaks in poorer parts of the country but also in places like university hostels. Northland, hit hard by an epidemic of the B strain in the nineties and early 2000s, had an outbreak of meningococcal C disease in 2011 that led to the region's health board instituting a widespread and successful vaccination campaign to stop it.

Although some of the factors that tipped the balance to start those epidemics of meningococcal disease have changed, poverty, overcrowding and poor housing continue to contribute to an unacceptably high incidence of preventable childhood disease. This is both debilitating for children and their families but also hugely costly to our communities, and to you and me who ultimately fund our health and social services.

Winter brings an enormous influx of sick kids into our hospital. Of those with chest infections, most live in cold, damp, overcrowded houses. Our intensive care unit has a paediatric wing, which in winter is full most of the time. In there are little babies with respiratory infections from viruses with strange names like respiratory syncytial virus, influenza, parainfluenza, enterovirus and rhinovirus. These infections are also spread through droplets by coughing and sneezing.

One of the most prevalent illnesses caused by these viruses has a strange name—bronchiolitis: -itis means inflammation; bronchioles are the very small airways in our lungs; hence inflammation affecting the small airways. As a result of the inflammation, air that is easily breathed in cannot all be breathed out due to the inflamed airways. This leads to the chest becoming hyperinflated, making it harder and harder for kids to breathe. In the main, infants and young children are nose breathers and this disease will also make them snotty, further increasing their difficulty in breathing. Children who are strong and healthy can usually put up with this for longer and will do much better than smaller babies and those born prematurely.

When we began the round in the ICU one winter morning a few years ago, I recognised Margretta immediately. She was embarrassed to be back with her seven-month-old son—his sixth hospital admission with bronchiolitis. She worried that we would think she was a bad mum and that Rikki would be taken away from her. Despite our lobbying, their large family still lived in the same cold house.

Rikki, a small baby, was breathing hard and fast, his head bobbing with each breath. The monitor said 80 breaths a minute but still with a good oxygen saturation of 96 per cent. Once he was wrapped snugly in a colourful blanket, I slid in an IV, then took some bloods to send to the lab and a swab from the back of his nose to send for virology. One nurse steadied his head as another used a small suction catheter to clear out Rikki's blocked nose. They then slipped in a nasogastric tube to keep his tummy empty so it wouldn't press against his diaphragm and make his breathing even more difficult. Finally, he had another chest X-ray. Rikki didn't like any of that—nor did his breathing.

Our next move was to make him drowsy with an old-fashioned drug called chloral hydrate, which we put down his nasogastric tube, and then we put him on bubble CPAP (continuous positive airway pressure).

Bubble CPAP is a simple, non-invasive way to support babies who are struggling to breathe. It delivers humidified oxygen to the child via a pair of soft nasal prongs. The expiratory limb of the circuit carrying the baby's expired gas is placed in a reservoir open to air but under water at a depth of between 1 and 10 centimetres of water, thereby generating between 1 and 10 centimetres of continuous positive pressure in the breathing circuit.

It is incredible to see the relief this brings to these infants working so hard to breathe. As soon as we put Rikki on, now more sleepy and cooperative thanks to that small dose of chloral hydrate, his respiratory rate settled and his breathing required much less effort. Not only did he look more settled but so did we.

A good number of babies are admitted to hospital more than once each winter, and we will see those same children many times throughout their infancy. Unsurprisingly, those born either very small or prematurely seem to be at greatest risk of deterioration.

What we do in the hospital, giving oxygen and antibiotics and putting kids on ventilators, treats the end result but does nothing to address the causes of this recurring problem. Nor does the advice of well-meaning, prestigious people like the former Chief Medical Officer of the UK, who gave this advice to the people of Britain in 1999:

1. Don't smoke. If you can, stop. If you can't, cut down.
2. Follow a balanced diet with plenty of fruit and vegetables.
3. Keep physically active.
4. Manage stress by, for example, talking things through and making time to relax.
5. If you drink alcohol, do so in moderation.
6. Cover up in the sun, and protect children from sunburn.
7. Practise safer sex.
8. Take up cancer screening opportunities.

9. Be safe on the road: follow the Highway Code.
10. Learn first aid ABC—airways, breathing, circulation.[1]

Advice like this is easy to give and, in this case, I'm sure it was well meant. Others are less generous about the causes of ill health, blaming those individuals who fill our hospital wards, keep coming back to our emergency departments, or use our social services. We've all heard the rhetoric: 'They are lazy.' 'Why don't they get a job?' 'They don't care.' 'They don't love their children.' 'They don't try hard enough.'

Soon after the CMO's message to the people of Britain, I attended a talk in Wellington delivered by Ichiro Kawachi, a professor of Public Health at Harvard. He gave recommendations of a different sort. His advice for staying healthy differed, playing on the delusion that the queues at the doors of our social services were the result of poor choices. He urged:

1. Don't be poor. If you can, stop. If you can't, try not to be poor for too long.
2. Don't have poor parents.
3. Don't live in a poor neighbourhood.
4. Own a car.
5. Practise not losing your job and don't become unemployed.

Ichiro points to many of the structural and social issues that need to be addressed if we are to have a more equal society. He also made it clear that, try as they might, many people need to be given a hand up and out of the hole they find themselves in. This is not the same as being forced out of one hole and into another.

When I was the Principal Medical Advisor to the Minister of Health and the Director General of Health, I schlepped up and down from Auckland to Wellington every other week. While there, I was given a hat to wear—across its hatband was written the letters 'WoG'. Hmm, yes, I was. 'WoG' stood for 'Whole of Government'. The hat was a reminder to members of the Ministry of Health executive team that we should be working more collaboratively with other agencies to address the complex real life problems we were faced with. Sadly, on its own that symbolic action was not enough—'hat and hope' was not a plan.

The barriers to this kind of transformative thinking and activity are many and significant. Budgets and agendas continue to be jealously protected within government departments, and our world continues to be ruled by the same old thinking that allows the problems we face to persist. As a result, the well-meaning, stroboscopic interventions of the public service continue and most of the root causes that drive our concerns remain unaddressed.

As for the hat, it quickly became my much needed protection from the sun, worn exclusively in the privacy of my own garden.

Hospital management is expensive and complex. However, this cost and complexity can be rationalised by the provision of good information about the changing demand for services. Middlemore, like many other modern hospitals, utilises historic data to accurately predict the changing demand for services across all of its departments. As part of that, a hospital status report is generated each day and more often than not it looks like this:

TODAY THE HOSPITAL IS FULL
—107 per cent of capacity

- Currently there are 100 patients in the Emergency Department of which 50 are waiting for an inpatient bed.
- There are 8 over-census patients in treatment rooms around the medical wards.
- There are 8 patients in the Gastro Clinic.
- There are 7 female adult patients in Kidz First Short Stay Unit.
- There are a further 17 patients expected in Day Surgery, 5 will require beds.
- The Discharge Lounge in Wd 34 E is full with 4 inpatients and this has the potential to delay discharges from Surgical Services today.
- There are 5105 minutes of acute surgery needing to be done and 34 patients are currently waiting.
- There were 298 patients through the emergency department yesterday, similar numbers are expected today.
- Nursing shortages as a result of sick leave are an issue.

The adult wards at my hospital are usually full but now, increasingly, with younger people suffering from life threatening complications of type 2 diabetes—a largely preventable disease associated with obesity.

Despite all the good things we have achieved as a nation why is it that we are not doing better at preventing the preventable? Should this not embarrass us? Does this not cost the health system millions of dollars and effectively prevent many people from making a productive contribution to their families, communities and our nation?

'Of course' is the answer to all of those questions!

Preventing disease requires a whole of society approach and ought to start with the well-being of families, pregnant women and children. During my time working in Samoa, I frequently did ward rounds with the paediatricians. All women, they were hard working, very skilled and capable of doing amazing things with not very much.

In the middle of a round one morning, a child came into the emergency department with an obvious problem with her breathing. She was two years old and had been unwell for two weeks, during which time she had been treated by traditional healers. We heard her before we saw her—a rhythmic high pitched squeaking noise with each breath, accompanied by an in-drawing visible at her throat and a sucking in of her abdomen in an effort to get air into her lungs. That noise is called stridor. It results from a narrowing of the airway at some point as air makes its way from the mouth to the upper trachea. Until an effective vaccine was introduced a little over twenty years ago, the commonest cause of stridor was epiglottitis—an infection of the epiglottis caused by a bacteria called *Haemophilus influenzae*.

The epiglottis itself is a strange U-shaped structure that lives deep in the throat and effectively guards the opening of the larynx, protecting us from inhaling our food as we swallow.

The child's name was Vaelua, and she weighed only 8 kilograms. Vaelua had a temperature of 40 degrees Celsius and looked pale. I spoke to her then I prodded her, but she didn't respond. She was already unconscious because of the build-up of CO_2 in her blood. A lateral X-ray of her neck done earlier did not suggest epiglottitis but instead showed an enormous bulge of soft tissue clearly narrowing her airway around her larynx. It was also obvious that if we didn't do something soon, Vaelua would stop breathing and die. That something had to be inserting a breathing tube into her airway to bypass the obstruction; but in emergency situations like this, fraught with danger, that can be next to impossible.

The principles of treatment in cases like this are to disturb the child as little as possible in case we lose the airway completely. Our priority is to get them to a skilled anaesthetist and surgeon in the operating theatre. Once there, we know from experience that the safest course of action is to keep the child breathing on their own while inhaling an anaesthetic vapour until they are deeply asleep. This allows the anaesthetist to see whether they can visualise the larynx and then insert a breathing tube past the obstruction.

I called the theatres and told them we were on our way. En route to the theatre suite, we pushed past people in corridors, ejected others from lifts and politely ignored the theatre orderly's instruction for me to change into scrubs. To have done so would have cost Vaelua her life.

Once in theatre we followed the rules, but soon after arriving the child simply stopped breathing. The amount of oxygen in her blood dropped precipitously and her heart rate slowed dramatically. Our anaesthetist looked into Vaelua's mouth to see whether we might get the breathing tube in from the top end but all he could see were swollen folds of tissue. As my colleague Dina began CPR, I looked toward Aleki, our surgeon, and together we talked him through his first ever emergency tracheostomy—a vertical incision in the neck, down through the strap muscles to expose the trachea, then one final slit into it to allow for the passage of the breathing tube.

I reckon the whole thing took no more than two or three minutes from the time she stopped breathing to the point where the tube was in and her life saved. We attached the tube to a ventilator bag and puffed 100 per cent oxygen into her lungs. As we did this, Vaelua's heart rate rose and the oxygen saturation in her blood returned to a very healthy 100 per cent. Having secured the tube, we gave her antibiotics. Then using a syringe and needle, through her widely open mouth, we punctured into the abscess cavity and removed 70 millilitres of foul-smelling brown pus.

Vaelua came back to the ICU after that and remained on a ventilator for a couple of days to allow the swelling in her neck to go down. Then, on the third morning, we removed the breathing tube from the tracheostomy hole in her neck, covered it with gauze and tape and off she went, breathing normally again through her mouth and nose. Three days later, Vaelua went home.

Kids are definitely not small adults. Although we have the same bits—spleen, kidney, bone and brain—these organs do different things for us at different times of our lives; they can change shape as the child grows and respond differently in illness when we do things to them. The airway of a child is a case in point—small and narrow, the structures there are floppy and the relationships they have with each other are different. For those of us used to dealing with adults, all this can make for trouble. We did well with Vaelua. Yes we were lucky, but we were also prepared.

We know that many childhood diseases occur in our poorest households. The causes for this are not that complex or complicated. Putting wind behind Ichiro Kawachi's sails is the transformative thinking behind the report 'Solutions to Child

Poverty in New Zealand' released by the Office of the Children's Commissioner in December 2012.[2] Far from thinking that improving health is reliant on new technology or more doctors and a massive investment in new pharmaceuticals, the report recommended making moderate investments in four key areas. Namely, pay people a living wage, provide better housing, make nutritious food affordable and keep kids engaged at school. What a treat for a government to have such an expert group as this help with such an important issue. What a travesty the government of the day didn't have the humility to accept those recommendations and the good sense to act on them.

In 2008, in a particularly poor part of Auckland, in a community of many single parents and large families, something really wonderful began. It started with a group of primary school teachers who had been struggling to bring their kids up to speed with simple reading, writing and arithmetic. Instead of arriving at school with a five-year-old's reading level, most came with the reading level of a three-year-old. As a result, if they were to succeed at school these children would, in effect, need to learn at 1.5 times the pace of their peers. The teachers began an organisation called Manaiakalani that promoted learning in this impoverished community.

I met a group of these children in 2011 when they came to perform at the opening of Ko Awatea—a centre focused on health system innovation and improvement—on the campus at Middlemore Hospital. So here they were three years on leading a hilarious and, at the same time, moving performance of soliloquy, song, dance and storytelling that left the audience in stitches of laughter and in complete awe. These kids, once virtually illiterate, were now in command of their own destinies, connected to each other and the wider world to an extent that was simply mind-boggling. The children were passionate about learning and since then they, and other kids who have followed them, have gone on to achieve in all aspects of life.

> Manaiakalani draws a whole range of magnificence to it. Children passionate about learning and now doing significantly better on national assessments. Parents willing to make sacrifices and invest in their kids like never before; teachers and schools prepared to disrupt what they've always done to enable student learning; community, philanthropic, commercial and government partners willing to invest. Why? Because Manaiakalani is profoundly different and making a difference. The programme is new and exciting, and enabling a shift and acceleration in student achievement.
>
> —*Pat Snedden, Manaiakalani chair*

The work of the Manaiakalani Education Trust (www. manaiakalani.org) is a wonderful example of the potential all children have to succeed. It has shown that given the right guidance and assistance all children can do well, and that parents, no matter their circumstances, want the best for their children and will make sacrifices to ensure that they might succeed. Giving these children the chance to do that through learning will improve their health status as they age. It will also influence how they, in turn, will parent by showing them the importance of education and keeping their own kids healthy. This is how we will break the cycle of failure, of truancy and of illness.

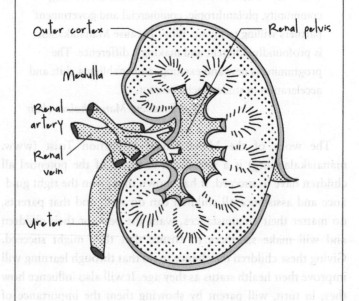

The kidney–

far too clever an organ to eat!

MY COLLEAGUES IN THE ICU are a terrific lot, patient and forgiving. As a group we are extraordinarily tight and I can say, hand on heart, that we genuinely like each other and take an interest in each other's lives. That is just as well because we spend a lot of time together and rely on each other to provide the 24/7 services our patients demand. Our lives are ones of constant compromise—'Can you do my Thursday if I do your Saturday?' 'One of the kids is sick so could you do my second on today, please?' The hospital has been a second home and, given the nature of our work, we all have a second family to think about. When I look around at other groups cast together for a lifetime like us, we have done well.

Like all families though, there are times when we drive each other crazy. This worries us because we're sensitive people and generally attuned to each other's feelings. I especially worry about it because I'm high maintenance on one or two fronts because of the huge range of things I do and the chaos which comes when I don't manage them well.

Thankfully, we are all somewhat protected from each other by the regular, six-monthly turnover of registrars. These young doctors are wanting to be specialists in anaesthesia, emergency medicine or general medicine, so they move through different departments every six months to cover off their training requirements. Of course, we try to convert as many of them as possible to become trainees with the College of Intensive Care Medicine.

These young ones are hard-working and conscientious. They are very bright and most are quite savvy in a streetwise kind of way so they're able to adapt to the intricacies of working in different parts of different hospitals, all of which have their own unique cultures and personalities.

I love hearing the registrars chat, all the while getting a sense of how they see the world—our one and their one. It's really just gossip most of the time interspersed with occasional deeply philosophical arguments about the purpose of life. Sometimes they make me feel very old, but sometimes they sound old themselves and I feel sorry for them.

These young people bring fresh ideas and as a group we welcome that. Without their banter and our need to teach and supervise them, I am sure some of my colleagues would have given up on me years ago.

For many years I greeted these young doctors with a range of questions. I am genuinely interested in them as people. I'm also keen to learn about why they are doing what they are doing, and what they hope to accomplish in the future. I also like to ask them whether they eat kidneys.

You may think that is a strange question. If you do, I would either invite you to come and spend some time with us in the ICU or it might be slightly simpler if you read on . . . .

I have a habit of anthropomorphising the organs of the body. That's why I see the heart as reliable and organised in its function but capable of such stupidity in how it keeps going in some and how it stops in others. Contrast that with the unimaginably clever kidney, which some people choose to eat. I simply cannot and will not because I have too much respect for it as an organ and so too should those young kidney-eating doctors! I say the same thing about the brain and the liver of course, although there is a complication there. The liver is so brilliant an organ I know I should feel the same way but I am Jewish and 'chopped liver' (chicken livers) is a cultural imperative for me—in much the same way foie gras is to the French. When I explain that to the young doctors, trying to hide my smile, some roll their eyes while others appear dumbfounded.

I asked the same question in Samoa. 'Yes, of course we do!' was the answer. It is a sign of respect and honour to be a guest at a Sunday lunch with a Samoan family. Sundays in this proud independent island state are like the Sundays of old where devotion to G-d and family are unparalleled. The day starts early to prepare the umu—Samoa's equivalent of the Māori hāngī. Traditional foods and delicacies are placed in the earth oven to cook while the family attend church. The pièce de résistance is, of course, the whole pig, named Babe by many. Different parts of the pig are allocated to the assembled diners according to their status. Offal including the liver, heart and *kidney* are offered to the village chief or matai, as too is the tuala of the pig—that part of the body on the back between the ribs and the pelvis. The belief is that there is power in those organs and that power is assumed by those lucky enough to be offered it.

On occasions I too was offered the tuala of the pig, a potentially tricky situation for a Jewish man like me. Thankfully I was brought up by pork-eating Jewish parents who only ate kosher pork from circumcised pigs killed facing Jerusalem. So out of respect I accepted the honour with grace and a smile.

In the great debate between creationists and scientists over the origins of the world, the former argue that the world and man were created by G-d in seven days; the latter believe that mankind evolved over billions of years. Of course, I am clearly with the scientists on this one. However, in my heart, I would like to think that we are something more than just another form of animal life constantly evolving to become something else again.

When I think about the kidney, knowing what I know about how it functions and has adapted, I am left dumbfounded by its intricacies. There is no way such a complex and reliable thing could have been created in seven days, but it's also hard for me to accept there is not some divine hand behind its evolution over such a long a time.

For many years, I spent time looking after the health of British tourists injured overseas. When I started, I would do ward rounds to all corners of the world from a small office in West Sussex.

As a guide I used a large white board and then later a new revolutionary tool, an Amstrad computer with its weird alien green font on a black background, to keep track of them all and to make my notes.

My patients, mostly domiciled in the UK, were scattered across all four corners of the world and suffered from a variety of ailments and injuries. It was my job to liaise with their treating medical teams to determine what levels of treatment were appropriate and to help decide when they were safe to travel home. Some of the travellers could do that on their own, others needed medical escorts—sometimes a nurse, sometimes a doctor. A few needed urgent attention so a team would be sent to oversee their care and bring them home on a commercial airliner or in an air ambulance. I did most of those trips and had the chance to witness how differently the same condition was treated in different parts of the world. It was a fun and challenging role and I learned to be extremely resourceful, often doing a lot with not very much.

Whether we are black or white, speak French or English, grew up in the northern hemisphere or on the other side of the world, when we look under the skin, into the blood circulating around our bodies, into our organs and deep down into the protoplasm of each and every cell, we are essentially the same. That came to me as an epiphany in the operating room of a small hospital in Malaysia. My London-based patient was from the Caribbean and had been gravely injured in a car crash on the motorway from Kuala Lumpur to Malacca. Back then I was young and perhaps a bit thoughtless so now feel embarrassed about the epiphany I had on seeing the pink mesentery of his intestine—pink like mine and pink like yours!

Our kidneys all look the same too. We have two, each weighing about 150 grams and running to 12 to 14 centimetres in length. They live in the area behind the abdominal cavity that we call the retroperitoneum, on either side of our bodies just below the level of the ribs. The kidneys have an outer cortex, a medulla and a renal pelvis, where urine begins its journey down the ureter into our bladder and from there, into the loo or under a tree in the garden.

That journey belies the complexity of the process—bulk filtration, selective reabsorption of fluid and molecules, and secretion of wastes. In a series of self-adjusting processes determined by a myriad of feedback loops, normal kidneys work hard to restore us to homeostasis no matter our circumstance.

These horseshoe-shaped organs keep us well by continually cleaning our blood of the rubbish created by the messy business of living. They do this by constantly regulating the fluid and electrolyte balance in our bodies. In order to carry out that task, they receive an enormous blood flow via each renal artery.

Adults have about five litres of blood in circulation at any one time. Of that, two litres are red blood cells and three litres are plasma. Every day the kidneys filter 180 litres of plasma at the staggering rate of 120 millilitres per minute! The functional unit of the kidney that does this is the nephron and each kidney has a million nephrons. If attached end to end, our supply of nephrons would be 160 kilometres long.

Each nephron is a complex little beast made up of different parts. There are a series of buckets and tubes into which fluid flows. The nephron's interface with the blood is the Bowman's capsule in which sits the glomerulus. The Bowman's capsule is located in the outer cortex of the kidney. This glomerulus is a strange tangle of small capillaries where fluid and molecules are forced down a pressure gradient to form what we call the glomerular filtrate. This filtrate enters the Bowman's capsule then runs into the proximal convoluted tubule, where about 70 per cent of the filtered plasma water and sodium is reabsorbed together with all the glucose and amino acids. From there, the filtrate travels into the ascending and descending loop of Henle, which are located in the medulla of the kidney, water is reabsorbed and our electrolyte balance fine-tuned. This effluent then flows into a final distal tubule deeper in the medulla for more water to be reabsorbed or secreted, a final check and then voilà, we have urine appear in the renal pelvis and soon after in the ureter running down into the bladder and when it suits into the loo—it's amazing, isn't it! So no matter how many pints we drink in the pub or how much salt or other minerals we ingest with our food, our kidneys will sort it out for us.

The ability of the human kidney to adjust to changing circumstances is extraordinary, especially when it comes to dealing with cold or hot climates by conserving water when we are dehydrated. But the prize for efficiency of this process goes to the kangaroo rat and the camel. They both have extremely long loops of Henle and are capable of concentrating their urine down to the point it is almost solid.

Kidney failure is a disaster and, depending on the cause, can either be temporary or permanent. In the acute setting, kidney failure is usually caused by a constellation of factors including the impact of the disease process and how well (or not) the kidneys function normally. However in this setting, which is very different to that of patients with longstanding diabetes or other diseases specifically of the kidney, if the patient survives their acute illness or injury, the kidneys will usually recover their function within a period of two to four weeks. I say *if* the patient survives, because no matter the nature of the underlying problem, if it results in acute kidney failure there is an increased likelihood of death resulting. The reason for this is not obvious— acute kidney failure can be treated effectively with dialysis, so the increased mortality associated with it must be related to the severity of the disease process causing renal failure as well as a lot more damage to other body systems.

If the kidneys do fail acutely, without an interim period of dialysis, patients will usually die as a result of the metabolic effects associated with a loss of kidney function. Although it is life-saving, dialysis can be tricky in this unstable patient group.

Last century, I worked for a few years in one of London's oldest teaching hospitals. Now called the Royal London, there was nothing royal about it in the mid-1980s when it was just called the London Hospital. Set on the Whitechapel Road in east London, the hospital was one of those dark brick Victorian institutions, whose claim to fame was that it had the skeleton of Joseph Merrick, aka the Elephant Man, in its anatomy museum. It had history, that place, played out in all manner of ways including the plumbing.

Opposite it was the Grave Maurice (pronounced Morreece) pub and another 100 metres east of that, the Blind Beggar, where the Kray Brothers shot Jack 'The Hat' McVitie. Further east still was the Mile End Hospital, an annex of the London, not so far away as the crow flies but given the nature of the hospital telephone exchange in times of crisis, it might well have been on the other side of the world.

At Aldgate, just west of the hospital, was Blooms, a Jewish deli where we went for salt beef sandwiches and latkes. Mrs Bloom, hair done in the style of the Iron Lady, guarded the till, her face pinched tight as a snare drum from too many procedures. Just north of there was Brick Lane, famous for its curry houses, bagels and beer. A bit further north was London Fields where we lived.

'See one, do one, teach one' was the principle that guided service delivery at the hospital. It was a time when service trumped supervision and when junior doctors learned from their mistakes more frequently than they did from the things they did right. One day I was with a specialist seeing how to anaesthetise a patient for a coronary bypass graft, the next day I was performing the same procedure, and the day after I was an expert. It was crazy stuff. The workload was ferocious and the rosters cruel so every second week I did 134 hours on call.

The people were great though, including most of the double-dipping consultants who spent so much time in Harley St or the Princess Grace, a private hospital in upmarket Marylebone. Often they would ask us to help them. Having another set of hands meant they could get through five or six cardiac cases in a day instead of three. At the end of each procedure, I'd take the still anaesthetised patients to the ICU as the boss started the next one. For my trouble, each time I helped I was given 50 pounds.

I will never forget my first day on my own in the cardiac theatre at the London. The patient was a bus conductor from Newham. He was only 5 foot 3, bald and of a wiry build. He was having a quadruple bypass and a mitral valve replacement because his leaked badly.

Operating theatres are like a stage and the different contributing staff like actors, with each day bringing a new performance. Back then, the performance began in the theatre itself with the anaesthetist inserting an arterial line usually into the radial artery, where you feel for the pulse in the right wrist. This was used primarily to check the patient's blood pressure and allowed for frequent blood tests to be taken to monitor the patient's state. The anaesthetic technician then attached the ECG leads and finger probe of the oximeter to measure the oxygen saturation of their blood. Then we put the patient off to sleep, taking great care with our choice and doses of drugs.

The arterial line slid in beautifully, he went to sleep with no change in his blood pressure or heart rate, and when I tipped him head down to insert three long intravenous catheters into his internal jugular vein, they went in first time too. I was on a roll. The different actors played their part, lines were spoken and things that needed to be done were done well.

The play continued and he went onto the bypass machine without difficulty. This machine that assumes the role of the heart and the lungs is made up of different components including a large cannula inserted into the right atrium of the heart, from where venous or blue blood is drawn into the machine by a centrifugal pump. A set of roller pumps then propels the blood around a circuit made of silicone to an oxygenator, which adds oxygen to the blood and removes carbon dioxide before finally returning that oxygen-rich red blood via another cannula inserted by the surgeons into the aorta. When the perfusionist who operates the bypass machine, the surgeon and the anaesthetist speak together it reminds me of listening to air traffic controllers—there's a lot of words but there doesn't seem to be any obvious meaning!

Once on bypass, the surgical team then stops the beating heart by infusing a cold, potassium-rich cardioplegic solution into the coronary arteries. This makes it easier for them to operate on the heart's bits and pieces, putting new grafts around old blockages and inserting new valves to replace worn-out old ones.

While one surgeon took the large saphenous vein from his leg, another prepped the heart; he received four grafts around obstructions in his coronary arteries and a new mechanical heart valve that would forever go clickety-click inside his chest so long as he lived. All was good until we warmed him up to get his heart started and off the bypass machine. Each time we tried to do this, we failed. His heart was too weak to fully take over. This wasn't in the script.

The surgeon stared at me as though it was my fault. I spoke to him but he didn't answer. I called for help and, in the meantime, put up an infusion of drugs to help the patient's heart. On the fourth attempt, we finally got him off the bypass machine but all was not well.

His heart was limping as we raced to the ICU. It was a Friday afternoon and I was on for the entire weekend. The unit was full—people with overdoses, a couple of victims of a bad car crash, and three other cardiac cases that had been done that day and the day before. My boss for the night had long since gone and would not be back until the next morning but was available by phone.

The bus conductor was struggling. I spoke with his wife and she cried. Over the next few hours, his heart rhythm settled down and his blood pressure improved—but he wasn't peeing and that was bad. The bag attached to his catheter had only 100 millilitres of urine in it after five hours in theatre. His initial blood tests showed a significant deterioration in his renal function and he was requiring more oxygen from the ventilator than I expected. Most likely this was the result of what had happened toward the end of the case when he had a particularly low cardiac output, injuring his kidneys and also causing fluid to accumulate in his lungs.

I was young and I was worried. I was worried because if his kidneys failed he would need dialysis and, although we could do that, the risk of him dying was significantly increased. I wanted to give him more fluid but thought that his heart might not stand that and his lung function would worsen. I rang the boss for advice and then began to fiddle. A bit more fluid, a bit more pressure from the ventilator, some drugs to ensure he had decent blood pressure, a dose of frusemide—a diuretic to make him pee—and a few other manoeuvres for good measure.

Although the exact detail now escapes me, I know I spent much of that night sitting on a stool beside the bus conductor's bed counting drops of urine as they leaked one by one into his catheter bag, smiling as the drips slowly turned into a trickle and, by morning, into a torrent. In the end he did well. About a year later, I saw him conducting on the number 22 bus that ran from Hackney to the West End. He recognised me and doffed his enormous conductor's hat in my direction and I returned the doff with a smile.

Many patients who develop overwhelming organ failure from acute illness or injury will develop kidney failure and, without dialysis, they will die. This happens in the same way as someone who had become hypoxic as a result of extreme breathing difficulties would die without respiratory support, or someone might die from shock if they aren't resuscitated with intravenous fluid and drugs to support their cardiac function. If we don't deal with the underlying cause of all that mayhem, people die.

Roger was 51 and normally well. He was married to Rosalie and they had two kids, aged fourteen and sixteen. Roger had no medical issues that he knew about, didn't smoke and had only been in hospital for a reconstruction of his left knee, which he'd injured playing rugby a long time before. He was a fit guy. I have no real explanation as to why he became so ill and almost died from a simple skin infection; why he got it is still a mystery to me.

Roger was on a plane heading to Auckland from Australia when the redness and pain started. His leg was itchy so he scratched it. By the time he arrived in Auckland he was hot, sweaty and already delirious. Paramedics met him at the gate. Recognising how ill he was, they gave him oxygen to breathe, put in an IV line, and raced him to Middlemore Hospital. I first saw Roger in the resuscitation room of the ED.

He was now barely conscious, had a temperature of 40 degrees Celsius, was breathing hard, and both the oxygen level in his blood and his blood pressure were dangerously low. So too was his blood sugar level. On his leg was the cause of all this—a spreading redness extending from the shin to the mid-thigh. He had a cellulitis, an infection of the skin causing what we define as septic shock. This is the result of an overwhelming infection from bacteria that have spread into his blood stream now causing havoc with his other organs.

The redness working its way up Roger's leg was just the tip of something much bigger and more deadly: he was at war with a bacterium called *Staphylococcus aureus* and the exotoxin it produces. These poisonous substances circulate in our blood stream, destroying cells and disrupting our normal cellular mechanisms. One organ down, another quickly following, Roger was in a bad way.

When people become acutely ill, the immediate threat to their life is from a failure of their respiratory and cardiovascular systems so that's where we started. Oxygen by mask, soon after via a tube into his trachea, driven by an expensive ventilator; fluids in the vein and high doses of drugs to prop up his flagging circulation; glucose to prevent the disastrous damage to the brain that results from prolonged hypoglycaemia; antibiotics to kill the bugs; low dose hydrocortisone to help everything; and a quick look-see in the operating room to ensure there was no deeper infection or necrotic material that needed to be debrided and removed. All of these interventions are urgent; unless they happen fast, people die. These things are obvious to me and to the people I normally work with; it's not to less experienced doctors or those who might see something like this once a year or once a lifetime. Delayed resuscitation and treatment not only increase the risk of death, but also lead to a need for more aggressive and protracted organ support. This in turn means a delayed recovery with more profound psychological and physical consequences for the patient on discharge from hospital.

Within an hour, Roger was on close to maximal therapy and off to the operating room for a 'keyhole procedure'. To define the extent and depth of the infection in his leg, the surgeons make a series of incisions to define the proximal extent of the infection—how far it has spread up the leg. Incisions are also made to determine the depth of infection, whether it is confined to the skin or if it involves deeper areas of the leg, like the subcutaneous fat, the fascia that overlies the muscle, or even the muscle itself. Dead tissue will never be cured by antibiotics alone and must be removed; if not it will be a source of ongoing infection and the patient will not get better. 'Heal with steel' and 'never let the sun go down on undrained pus' are two mantras for the successful treatment of people like this. The message is that antibiotics alone will not be enough; surgical drainage of pus and debridement of dead tissue is necessary to effect a recovery.

Members of the public and doctors unused to managing critical illness often worry that a patient could be so sick to go to the operating room. I usually reply that they are so sick they must go.

As it happened there was no dead tissue or pus in Roger's leg so we concentrated our fire on what we were already doing to effectively treat his evolving organ failure while continuing to marinate him in antibiotics. Despite this Roger's condition continued to get worse.

When I met with his family, they asked me a series of terrific questions including: What more could we do? Would he survive? What would his survival depend on? Why was he still getting worse if we knew what we were doing?

I did my best to explain again using the domino analogy. If our treatments were effective and we did no substantial harm by them, and if we were able to support Roger with our machines, and if he had the physical and physiological reserve and inner strength to withstand what was happening to him, he *might* get better. The dominoes would slowly stop falling. Then the rate at which we picked them up would start to exceed the rate at which they fell. If he recovered, those dominoes would shuffle themselves into lines again but never quite in the same order they'd been in before.

Roger's organs were going down fast. He was still on a venti- lator and needed high pressures and more and more oxygen. He was still being actively resuscitated with fluid and was on high doses of drugs to improve his circulation. His blood was not clotting and now his kidneys were not working.

Developing renal failure in this setting of acute illness makes recovery impossible without dialysis. In illnesses like this, although the kidneys usually will recover if the patient recovers—that may take two to three weeks—if we don't correct the worsening biochemical abnormalities in the patient's blood, the other organs of the body will simply shut up shop and slowly die, and the patient will follow. It's a bit like swimming in a horribly polluted river—if we stay in there long enough, we will die too.

In the late 1980s, Middlemore Hospital was the first inten- sive care unit in the country to use continuous renal replacement therapy for patients with acute kidney failure. Following the principles of intermittent dialysis—that form of dialysis used for four hours at a time, three to four times a week for patients with permanent end-stage renal failure from diseases like diabetes and glomerulonephritis (the disease suffered by Jonah Lomu)— continuous dialysis is deliberately prolonged, lasting up to eight hours a day and in this setting usually required every day to slowly and steadily clear the waste products generated by the body.

In those days, the technology was very different to what is available today. Back then, we used a system called the Hannover Balance where one large cannulae was placed in the femoral vein in the groin with another in the femoral artery so the flow of blood through the blood filter was effectively driven by the patient's own blood pressure. The pores on the filter were designed to allow molecules of a certain size to escape from the blood into an overflow while ordinary intravenous fluid was given as a replacement. The balance itself referred to an elaborate mix of weights and measures on a chrome frame to ensure we gave and took off the correct amounts of fluid and electrolytes. Setting it up took hours and the machine and necessary paraphernalia to make it work filled half a room.

Roger needed dialysis as well as those other organ supports to buy time in the hope that he would have the wherewithal to recover. Now dialysis is a simple affair and compared to early models, modern dialysis machines are simple and almost idiot-proof. These machines take blood from one lumen of a large-bore intravenous catheter in an internal jugular vein in the neck, or a subclavian vein in the chest, or a femoral vein in the groin, and return the cleansed blood to the body via a second lumen in the same catheter.

People like Roger are incredibly unstable so great care needs to be taken in doing all of this, especially in getting them on dialysis to avoid a cardiovascular collapse. The machines are smart and interactive and the process is extraordinarily gentle, allowing us to dial up very low flows of blood and dialysate fluid to keep patients stable.

Roger was on that machine for a solid 24 hours before it became evident that we were winning. His descent slowed and the deterioration in his numbers reached a nadir. Then he slowly began to improve.

Over the next few days we whittled away at the levels of support he was on. After a week, although still needing dialysis every second day, his breathing tube came out and he could talk with us. Like most ICU patients as sick as he was, he had few immediate memories of what had happened to him.

I reckon Roger was saved by that machine slowly whirring away in the background; it's modern, slick and understated and delivers what we call Slow Low Efficiency Daily Dialysis operating at a level well below what would be expected of just one human kidney, but enough to save a life.

The steady whirring of the roller pumps moving his blood at 200 millilitres per minute from the line in his femoral vein, through the filter and back to the same vein through the second lumen of the big catheter. Steadily too ran the dialysis fluid from the machine in an opposite direction to Roger's blood on the other side of the filter's membrane. All the time the steady passage of molecules across the filter left Roger's blood cleansed of the waste products normally cleared by his kidney.

Our organs operate best in the soup in which we were made. They struggle terribly in the poisonous mix that is renal failure so as this process continued, the drugs needed to support his blood pressure steadily reduced. Roger's fall slowed and after a nervous night it was clear that he was on the up. In his favour, Roger was young and he was healthy. He had been an athlete in his day and was still really fit despite those long sickle-shaped scars on both of his knees. If anyone was going to survive this kind of illness, it should be him.

Over the next few days, we weaned him off all of the drugs supporting his circulation and his requirement for ongoing intravenous resuscitation slowed then eventually stopped. His need for dialysis reduced from almost continuous to just once a day. All was heading in the right direction so we reduced his sedation and allowed him to slowly surface. Still drowsy and stunned he opened his eyes and responded appropriately to us. This was a great time for his family and for us too—for him to have gone so far and now to be seen to be coming back.

During those first few days, as we chased Roger as he tumbled toward death, we gave him 22 litres of fluid to help maintain a half decent blood pressure. If his kidneys had been working he would be peeing that out now but it would take two to three weeks for them to recover so we used our machine to take that fluid off him. Each day we took off between three and five litres. By the end of the week he was off the ventilator and breathing on his own.

A week later, he started to pee. Dilute urine, mostly water, came by the bucketful as his kidneys woke from their unconscious slumber. Slowly learning how to do its business all over again, the quality of his urine improved and its enormous quantities reduced. A week later, they were back on track. Those 12-centimetre fleshy horseshoes—forbidden fruit to me, a delicacy and honour to others—were away, and so too was Roger.

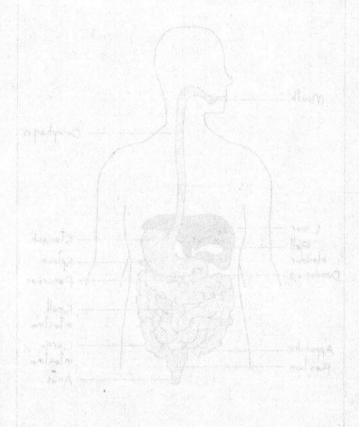

The Digestive Tract

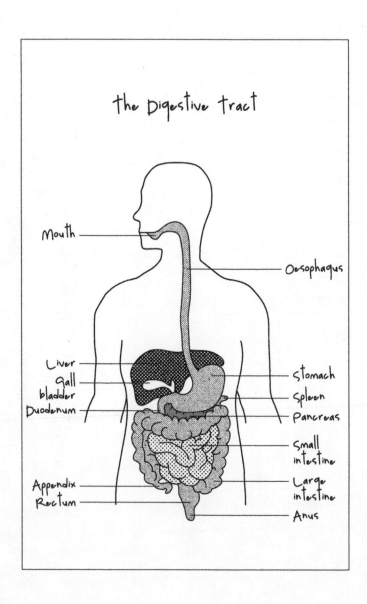

the Digestive tract

Mouth

Oesophagus

Liver

Gall
bladder

Duodenum

Stomach

Spleen

Pancreas

Small
intestine

Appendix

Rectum

Large
intestine

Anus

The modern day plague–

weighing us down

CHAPTER 4

The modern day plague

weighing us down

ONE NIGHT AT A reception, in a place 4000 kilometres from home, a lovely thing happened to me. Another guest, someone I recognised but couldn't quite place, thanked me for looking after his wife when she had been desperately ill. He was especially grateful for the time that I devoted to him and his family throughout that ordeal. That was twenty years ago when she was pregnant and suffering from a life threatening complication of pregnancy called the HELLP syndrome—a condition related to pre-eclampsia, whose name is an acronym of its three main features: haemolysis, elevated liver enzymes, and low platelet count.

Their child, their only child as it turns out, was delivered by caesarean section as much as anything to save the mother's life as well as that of the baby. That infant is now a student—tall and handsome too by the look of the photo he showed me. His wife, Wendy, is well and they are happy. Not long after her recovery, Wendy joined forces with another woman to start a support group to help other women in the same condition and to raise awareness of the warning signs of this condition. It was lovely to be reminded of that time.

It's always been hard to get into medical school and most students do so on the basis of their grades at college and their performance in an interview. The cut-off grade to get an interview is now so high that only the smartest and hardest working students get through. Once accepted these bright young things are separated from their peers and continuously fed with fact after intoxicating fact about physiology, anatomy, neuroscience, organ systems and their diseases, the heart, lungs and, yes, the kidney! They start early in the day and finish late at night. They study for exams and, because they don't meet anyone else, they often end up marrying each other. They go down roads others don't, take turn after turn into the middle of a maze that some never leave or recover from. This, combined with the extraordinary workload of many doctors, is the excuse I make when patients and their families complain about poor communication from medical staff, which leaves them feeling like they don't know what's going on.

It is easy to forget or not think about the impact we have on those we see on a daily basis. I have been stopped in supermarkets, on trains and planes, and in the street by people who I thought I had long forgotten about but, in the end, almost always remember. They remember me not primarily for my technical skills but for how I made them feel. More often than not, theirs are sad stories of loss that have, in time, become accepted. They remember that they were treated with dignity and respect, and they were listened to. Strangely, it is the sad stories that stay with me too. Probably because my emotional investment there is always so much greater.

I first saw Jake propped up on two beds in the emergency department. He had been brought into hospital with the help of the Fire Service who had to cut a bigger opening in the doorway of his house to carry him to the ambulance. He was only eighteen but weighed 280 kilograms.

Jake had been particularly unwell for three days with laboured breathing, most likely a consequence of a skin infection on his tree trunk-like legs. When I first saw him I struggled to get past a deluge of unhelpful thoughts about how he had come to be so big in order to concentrate on doing the right thing by this young man and his family. He was barely conscious, only mumbled when spoken to, and was not able to follow simple commands. Because his arm was twice the size of my thigh, getting a reliable recording of his blood pressure was difficult despite using the biggest cuff in the hospital. All the readings though were in the dangerously low range, as too was the level of oxygen in his blood measured by the pulse oximeter. As we made our assessments I had a brief but important conversation with his parents about the seriousness of the situation, learning more about Jake's life.

He was born with a rare but well-described condition called Prader-Willi syndrome, the result of a complex genetic abnormality in one of his chromosomes. Like many with the syndrome he suffered from polyphagia, an obsessive desire to eat, as well as a range of other behavioural and physical issues. Despite therapies and treatments throughout his childhood and adolescence, his obsessive behaviour became increasingly difficult to control and his weight gain accelerated.

Because of his size the paramedics couldn't find a vein to put in an IV line so that was left to me. As I lowered the head of Jake's bed to 30 degrees to put a line into the internal jugular vein in his neck, he quite suddenly stopped breathing and very quickly died. My lowering the bed, just a bit, was the final straw; 'expiratory airflow obstruction', we call it, or, to put it in layman's terms, Jake was effectively crushed by his own weight. Being so sick and so heavy, he simply didn't have the strength or drive to be able to activate and move his own respiratory muscles to breathe. When that happened we didn't try to resuscitate him. There was nothing we could do. It was an awkward and strange moment for those of us there trying to help him. Instead we immediately brought his family into the room to be with him as he faded away.

The cause of Jake's obesity was well known and with that came an acceptance by his parents of what might one day happen to their son. So, although a sad and tragic story for Jake and his family, the end was not unexpected. Nor did the family have unrealistic expectations of what we could do for him in hospital. At best, all we would offer was always going to be limited support with oxygen, fluids and antibiotics—that was our agreement. In the end, Jake was spared even the indignity of that, choosing to take himself off, hopefully to some better place.

While we can attribute the cause of Jake's size to a well-described genetic predisposition, what is fuelling the obesity epidemic worldwide is more complex. It is driven by a mix of factors that reflect changes in lifestyle—the burgeoning market economy, the advent and rapid spread of high-fat, high-sugar foods and drinks, mass marketing, urbanisation, changes in the labour market and much more. All these changes have swept across the world and they have effectively overwhelmed us. In many ways we have benefited by the massive global shifts of the late twentieth century and early twenty-first century, but in others, we have lost out.

Few countries or governments have been immune and fewer still have adapted to maximise the benefits of these changes and minimise their harms. Most have been simply swept along by them. We are, as a world, forever changed and to unpick some of this has become simply too hard for many to contemplate. However this epidemic, an unintended consequence of this post-industrial modern revolution, causes immense harm to individuals and creates huge costs for society. It simply must be addressed.

Seleni is a case in point. She, like millions of others, is enormous, weighing in at 160 kilograms, however, she was not born enormous. In fact, her mother remembers her as a slim child. When Seleni's hit adolescence that changed, when the impact of her diet and lifestyle began to take its toll. If she was thirsty, it was cool to drink a fizzy drink loaded with enormous amounts of sugar. If she was hungry, she would eat food high in carbohydrates and rich in fats. She would snack all day and at mealtimes eat large portions of whatever was being served. In the family home, the cupboards and shelves offered few healthy food choices, as did the shops nearby where she bought her food. Occasionally she would eat fruit and vegetables, but they were much more expensive to buy.

By the time Seleni was a teenager she weighed 120 kilograms. When she finished school at sixteen, she took a job as a seamstress. It suited her well because, by then, walking was uncomfortable and she got tired quickly.

Her mother, a big woman herself, remembers it was about then that she began to snore at night and nod off during the day. The snoring and daytime somnolence are signs of something we call sleep apnoea, a condition that results from a partial obstruction of our airway as we breathe.

It is common in overweight people and is characterised by cycles of loud snoring, periods of apnoea when no breathing occurs for short periods, and then commonly a very loud snore or grunt associated with the intake of another cycle of breaths. As unpleasant as this sounds for the sufferer, it is also deeply annoying for those forced to listen. If that was all it was, wearing earplugs, putting a pillow over your head, or sleeping in another room might help others put up with this. But the consequences for the sufferer are more sinister.

During these cycles of obstructed breathing and especially when Seleni's breathing stopped altogether, the oxygen saturation in her blood dropped to extremely low levels. Potentially dangerous in the moment, the cumulative effect of this degree of hypoxaemia causes physical changes in the arteries of the lung, leading to an increased resistance to blood pumped into the lungs by the right ventricle to pick up oxygen and dispose of carbon dioxide. In response, the right side of the heart becomes increasingly bulky, making it difficult for it to do its job. This cycle of increasing pulmonary vascular resistance and hypertrophy of the right side of the heart leads to a condition called pulmonary hypertension and, eventually, heart failure.

As bad as this sounds, it gets worse. Because of the weight of her chest wall whenever Seleni slept on her back she struggled to breathe adequately and couldn't effectively get rid of the carbon dioxide her body produced, a condition called obesity related hypoventilation, which accelerated her heart failure.

Like others with the same condition, Seleni complained about always being tired. She couldn't remember the last time she woke in the morning feeling refreshed or a time when she didn't doze off during the day. Just as well then that Seleni was a seamstress and not an airline pilot or bus driver.

Unfortunately her tiredness had other consequences too, making things much worse for her. Many of us will have had occasions where, through work or play, we've had a big night and not much sleep, leaving us tired the next day. With that often comes a ferocious appetite, usually for something hot and greasy like fish and chips—that's my weakness—or a meat pie. In my career as an intensivist, I have had many of those and know that the more tired I feel, the hungrier I become. There's a reason for that and it's called grehlin, 'the hunger hormone'.

Grehlin is released from the lining of the stomach as a response to this sort of tiredness. It works in the brain to increase our appetite as well as determining how quickly our hunger will return. Under normal circumstances, the effects of grehlin to stimulate appetite are matched by the impact of another hormone, leptin, which suppresses appetite. However, the impact of constant tiredness and a diet of high-sugar and high-fat food, both of which increase grehlin levels, are simply too much and we lose our balance.

Against this combination of market forces and physiology, Seleni didn't have a chance. She piled on more and more weight. Soon she weighed 140 kilograms. As that happened, her unwillingness to walk and exercise became a permanent disability, because of pain in her knees and a gnawing backache that never went away. By now she had high blood pressure. She was also diagnosed with diabetes when she had her first episode of cellulitis, a skin infection, in her fluid filled legs. Despite taking pills and testing her blood three times a day, Seleni's body was overwhelmed and she struggled to keep her blood pressure and sugar levels in the normal range.

The first time I met her was in the emergency department of my hospital. She weighed in at 160 kilograms and had come in with another bout of leg cellulitis, but this time complicated by a much more serious set of problems as a result of her diabetes.

To this point, obesity had been the defining feature of Seleni's life. Not only did it create health problems for her, it had an overwhelming influence on how she viewed herself as a person and it determined much of what she could and couldn't do in her everyday life. Obesity, then, had totally defined the quality of her life but now with the added complication of diabetes, it was the quantity of her life that was under direct threat.

Diabetes is a disease of our metabolism that is related to high levels of glucose in the blood. There are two common types of diabetes—type 1, or early onset diabetes, is most commonly diagnosed in children and teenagers, and type 2, or maturity onset diabetes, that usually affects those in middle age and the elderly. It is the latter form that is so common in people like Seleni.

Under normal circumstances, when we eat, our digestive tract breaks down carbohydrates—sugars and starches found in many foods—into glucose, a form of sugar that enters the bloodstream. That glucose is the fuel that keeps our cells alive and it is the hormone insulin, secreted from our pancreas, that allows us to absorb it and use it for energy. Diabetes develops when the body doesn't make enough insulin, or is not able to use insulin effectively, or both.

There is no doubt that obesity was the cause of Seleni's diabetes. Yes, perhaps she also may have had some kind of genetic predisposition to the disease but to overplay that card—as some do—is irresponsible and dangerous.

Like most people, Seleni was diagnosed when she presented to hospital with an inter-current infection although it is most likely that she would have had the disease for many months prior to that. If the cells of her body could talk, they would have told her far earlier than her doctor did because full-blown diabetes is usually preceded by a period of insulin resistance—a time when the cells of the body respond less and less to the effects of insulin. As a result, the pancreas pumps out more insulin in an attempt to overcome that resistance until finally it can't keep up and high blood sugar levels result. For Seleni and millions of others with this disease, the importance of protecting the body from high sugar levels cannot be overstated because the consequences of not doing so are dire.

Hyperglycaemia directly damages our major blood vessels: the aorta, carotid arteries, our coronary arteries and iliac and femoral vessels. It dramatically increases our risk of heart attack and stroke. It slowly wrecks the smaller arteries that take blood to the retinae of our eyes, resulting in what we call retinopathy; to our nerves, limiting their ability to transmit sensation— neuropathy; and to our kidneys—nephropathy. Diabetes is like a form of human rust slowly destroying us. Like many others before her, Seleni was rusty well before her diagnosis was made.

Weight loss, exercise and lifestyle changes will work for some and return their blood sugar levels to a more normal range. A select group might be offered more direct help to lose weight and undergo bariatric surgery, a range of different surgical procedures that have proven to be very effective in promoting significant weight loss among committed individuals, which can slow and, in some cases, cease the corrosion that diabetes causes. However, even if all the bariatric surgeons in the world operated 24 hours a day, seven days a week, this would hardly make a dent in the enormity of this problem. Hence most obese patients don't get this chance even though they simply cannot or will not be able to lose weight on their own. Seleni was one of those people. Her only realistic option was to continue on a course of therapy with drugs to control both her sugar levels and blood pressure in an attempt to minimise ongoing damage to her vessels and end organs, especially her kidneys.

On her most recent admission, the result of a severe infection in the soft tissues of her massive left leg, Seleni was much sicker than she had ever been. She was febrile, had low blood pressure and came in with a significant deterioration of her renal function due both to the progression of her diabetes and the impact of this acute infection.

To determine the extent and depth of the infection in her leg, Seleni went to the operating theatre where she was carefully anaesthetised. Once she was asleep, the surgeons did what we always ask them to do and assessed the viability of the tissues beneath the skin, starting at her ankle and working their way steadily to above her knee. What we saw was not pretty. Beneath the red and swollen skin, the subcutaneous fat and the muscles were a sick grey colour and they did not bleed when cut. This was the case from the ankle to the knee. In effect, her leg was dead so, to save her life, it was amputated above the knee.

During this time Seleni was in poor shape. She was asleep on a ventilator and receiving large volumes of resuscitation fluid and high doses of drugs to maintain an acceptable blood pressure. As soon as the surgery was over, she came back to the ICU where she immediately went onto a kidney dialysis machine to do the job of her failing kidneys.

Seleni eventually recovered, but although only 40, her kidneys—fatally damaged by uncontrolled diabetes and high blood pressure—never did. She was in hospital for several months before going home in a wheelchair to be cared for by her family and tied forever to the dialysis centre three times a week for the rest of her life.

Managing people of this size is difficult beyond description. On a practical level, everything is hard. Getting in an IV line, measuring blood pressure, doing a simple bedside examination, putting in a urinary catheter are all challenging and, in some cases, impossible. Moving the patient from one bed to another takes an army of people; getting appropriate investigations done can be limited by weight restrictions on CT and MRI tables and, even if you can get the scans done, the images can be hard to interpret. In addition there are personal prejudices that clinical staff need to acknowledge and overcome. There is a tendency to blame the patient for their condition and an acceptance that what will be will be, limiting the potential of what we might do to help and the success of any therapeutic intervention. These are real concerns best overcome by getting to know more about the person rather than being put off by their size.

Obesity and its consequences have become a public health emergency in much of the world. Recognised as a form of malnutrition, this crisis is more indolent but more lethal and costly than the malnutrition we are more used to seeing in poor nations across the world.

In many middle income nations, we now have in the same localities, notably our cities, both ends of that spectrum— babies transitioning from the breast who become increasingly malnourished because their food is of poor quality with few real nutrients, anorexic adolescents and young adults, and an increasing number of the morbidly obese.

People flock to urban areas in the Pacific, including those in New Zealand, in search of work, leaving their lands and their traditional family and cultural supports. These are the areas in which infant malnutrition and morbid obesity are on the rise. They bring with them a range of medical complications that are difficult to manage, as well as ethical and moral dilemmas about how our health and social services best respond.

Obesity is defined as an excessively high amount of body fat (adipose tissue) in relation to lean body mass and this is associated with a substantially increased risk of a number of health conditions.

Body mass index (BMI) is the most commonly used measure to classify underweight, overweight and obesity in both children and adults. BMI is a measure of weight adjusted for height and is calculated by dividing your weight in kilograms by your height in metres squared (kg/m^2).

International cut-off points for adults aged 18 years and over

Classification	BMI score (kg/m^2)	Risk of multiple diseases
Underweight	<18.50	Risk of other clinical problems increased
Normal range	18.50–24.99	Average risk
Overweight	25.00–29.99	Increased risk
Obese	≥30.00	High risk
Obese (class I)	30.00–34.99	High risk
Obese (class II)	35.00–39.99	Severe risk
Obese (class III)	≥40.00	Very severe risk

For children aged two to seventeen years, a similar set of BMI cut-off points have been developed by the International Obesity Task Force (IOTF).

People with an exceptionally low BMI from malnutrition are at risk from a wide range of clinical problems because they have little reserve to ward off illnesses and to heal themselves once they become sick or need an operation. That was shown to be the case in my own ICU when we looked at outcomes for patients admitted with a surgical diagnosis. Among surgical patients, those with a very low BMI generally do worse than those who have a very high BMI admitted for similar problems. At first I was surprised by that but the reason for it relates to the nature of the patients themselves—morbidly obese surgical patients are generally carefully selected and are coming for a specific surgical concern. Most won't have the advanced complications of end organ disease like Jake or Seleni and, if indeed they are admitted with organ failure as a result of their obesity, their treatment options are limited and their outcomes exceptionally poor.

The 2012/13 New Zealand Health Survey found that in the adult population:

- Almost one in three adults (aged fifteen years and over) were obese (31 per cent), with a further 34 per cent being overweight
- 48 per cent of Māori adults were obese
- 68 per cent of Pacific adults were obese
- Obesity in males had increased from 17 per cent in 1997 to 30 per cent in 2012/13
- Obesity in females had increased from 21 per cent in 1997 to 32 per cent in 2012/13.

When it comes to children, the same trends are emerging. The same health survey found that:

- One in nine children (aged two to fourteen years) were obese (11 per cent)
- A further one in five children were overweight (22 per cent)
- 19 per cent of Māori children were obese
- 27 per cent of Pacific children were obese
- Children living in the most deprived areas were three times as likely to be obese as children living in the least deprived areas. This finding is not explained by differences in the sex, age or ethnic composition of the child population across areas of high and low deprivation.
- The obesity rate in children has increased from 8 per cent in 2006/07 to 11 per cent in 2012/13.[3]

These are disastrous statistics for a small nation like ours struggling to provide health and social services from a small GDP (gross domestic product) that is growing only slowly.

New Zealand is not alone with this problem because obesity is an epidemic spreading largely unchecked across much of the developed world, with a doubling of the world-wide obesity rate since 1980.

According to the World Health Organisation, globally in 2014, more than 1.9 billion adults, eighteen years and older, were overweight. Of those, over 600 million were obese. It is affecting children in staggering numbers too, with 42 million children under the age of five now overweight or obese in 2013.[4]

This is the case too for most developing nations. It is a particular problem for small nation states like those in the Pacific where obesity rates are soaring and health services are already overwhelmed.

These numbers are now so high that obesity kills more people in the world than starvation or malnutrition, with those deaths being far more costly as nations shift scarce resources from other important public priorities.

Even though the causes of obesity are multiple it is a preventable disease. Proof of that are the many millions of individuals who are not obese and pockets of people who have the knowhow and the resources to organise themselves to stay healthy. Doing that at a national level requires a degree of stewardship that few governments wish to embrace because it requires a long-term commitment to effective public policy, social marketing and help to change the behaviours of communities, families and individuals. Some baulk and say it cannot be done and that we are at the mercy of the market and the media. I say bollocks to that.

Our future is what we are prepared to make it. Road trauma and tobacco use are just two examples of major threats to the health of the public where societies have made massive gains to reduce mortality and costs. The road toll has been lessened through effective public policy by licensing cars and drivers, designing safer roads and getting tough on drink driving. Tobacco-related deaths have been reduced through an increase in price and banning advertising of tobacco products. Certainly in the latter case the combination of regulation with social marketing, the availability of nicotine replacement therapy, and advice through the Quitline have been generally effective in reducing tobacco use among many groups. There is absolutely no reason why the same approach, over time, would not work with obesity. The major barrier to that is the antipathy and ignorance of many governments to use regulation to drive change—it simply doesn't sit well with their ideological beliefs and it would mean upsetting so many of their friends in the food and fat industry. As it stands, many nations are creating a future for themselves they will never be able to afford.

For Seleni—and so many like her—life as she knew it, or as she once hoped it would be, had gone forever, replaced by an exhausting and dangerous struggle just to stay alive. Perhaps looking on the bright side of life, at least half of those patients with diabetes will die of ischaemic heart disease, heart attack or stroke before their kidneys fail and they need dialysis. So perhaps Seleni has been lucky in that regard but her life on dialysis will be as hard as it will be short, with good odds that she will be dead in a year or two. Infection took out one of Seleni's legs—diabetes, heart failure and venous stasis from her obesity contributed to that. For many other diabetics, it is their neuropathy and a lack of sensation that leads to injuries to their feet, putting them at risk of infection. It could be something as simple as a tight shoe breaking the skin or a simple cut causing a wound that won't heal and eventually becoming infected. These small infections can quickly turn into a disaster, with more and more tissue being lost as the bugs spread in the encouraging environment of the diabetic foot and leg. Sometimes, after months of dressing changes and wound debridements, the foot or the leg is lost.

In many low- and middle-income countries where diabetes is endemic and resources and health services limited, wound care is often poor, leading to high rates of amputation. There are few prosthetics in those countries, leaving more and more people crippled and dependent on their families.

Looking in from the outside, it seems to me that obesity and diabetes are a man-made, modern version of the plague and I have no idea where that vortex of misery and cost will end up.

Given the reluctance of governments to act, we clinicians have both a collective and an individual responsibility to advocate for health policies to prevent the consequences of diseases like diabetes and its causes—especially obesity. Individually, we also have a responsibility to each patient to promote strategies to improve their health, keep them free of disease, and to help them stay well.

Each week, I spend time with a group of medical students. More often than not, my teaching is loosely structured as we talk about the people and the conditions they have seen that week. They are smart, keen to learn and seem to love those conversations.

Some are chatty, some more taciturn; some older, some younger. They vary in all sorts of ways, including their size. Priscilla is a fifth-year student and weighs 42 kilos—I know this not because I asked but because she told me! She weighs a little more than the amount of fluid we gave to Seleni over the first 48 hours of her descent toward death.

Sonny, a chatty, bright, fourth-year student, was exactly five times Priscilla's weight. He told me that one day after a class in which we had discussed the causes of obesity and its consequences. It was a conversation that I started with the class without initially thinking about him, but as soon as it began his body language quickly told me how uncomfortable it made him. He looked down and did not make eye contact with anyone and no one looked at him. He didn't say a word, and the conversation became stilted and difficult. Obviously, I should have spoken with him beforehand but I didn't.

Sonny was 22 and, once we were on our own, he was relieved to have the chance to talk. He lived with his sister, her child and their nanny. All of them in the house were overweight. Sonny had gout and was already a pre-diabetic. He had been admitted to hospital twice with infections related to his weight, but had not yet developed any major signs of organ failure. He had tried to lose weight on numerous occasions, often through starving himself, but always ended up hungry and bingeing on all the wrong foods. Each time he tried to lose weight, he put more on. If he lived somewhere else Sonny might have become a candidate for bariatric surgery but on this island that was impossible.

You don't get to be 210 kilograms by accident. Every day, he would drink four or five energy drinks, each containing fourteen teaspoons of sugar. In addition to that, he would also drink the same number of soft drinks, each with nine teaspoons of sugar. So each day Sonny would drink the equivalent of 100 teaspoons of sugar or 1600 calories.

He also ate what most people ate because it was available and cheap, foods with high carbohydrate and fat content: cream buns, two to three a day—another 900 calories; bread—520 calories; taro, often steamed then eaten with coconut cream and high-fat fried noodles. In between meals, he would snack on taro chips. His calorie intake was enormous and his energy expenditure through exercise minimal.

Later, I met with him and his sister and together we devised a plan for the household. First to go were the sugary drinks, replaced by water or niu (fresh coconut water). Sonny was a medical student, clever as they come and a master of the internet so with some urging he began to explore healthy food and snack options which he could turn to when he got hungry. With only a few hours research, he found a small range of healthy foods that were available and just affordable so over the next week he and his sister restocked their pantry. He even began to kept carrots and plain popcorn in his bag for emergencies.

Supported by his family and by me, in the first three weeks he lost 11 kilograms. His rate of weight loss has now slowed but he is heading in the right direction. Each week we meet, talk and think about the things that might trip him up. They will likely come from the people, places and things associated with his old lifestyle. They are everywhere and won't be going away. Sonny's goal is to get to 100 kilograms but that will be a stretch even if he sticks to his current plan. It will be hard and he will have his relapses but if he can stick with it, in time he will start to feel substantially better and be able to exercise more. With ongoing support, he might just get there and not become another Seleni but the odds remain stacked against that happening.

Looking across my career in medicine I have seen some extraordinary changes, including advances in technology allowing us to do complex things to many more patients safely and effectively. At the same time, the acuity curve of those we now treat in hospitals has shifted dramatically to the right, to the point where extraordinary effort and resources are directed to simply eke out a few more months of life for many already close to death. Seleni is now one of them, crippled to the point where she cannot work and contribute to the well-being of her family, community and society. She has sadly become a burden and a cost to those she loves and to the state for her ongoing care.

While well-off nations fiddle, the diabetes epidemic spreads and we spend more and more on medicines and hospital care to manage the rising tide of its complications. Low- and middle-income countries without the infrastructure or resources to do even this face an even more gruesome task, dealing with the septic complications of diabetes by draining abscesses and amputating limbs. Hospitals in those places are more houses of mutilation than healing. The world is spinning backwards and we are once again in the middle ages.

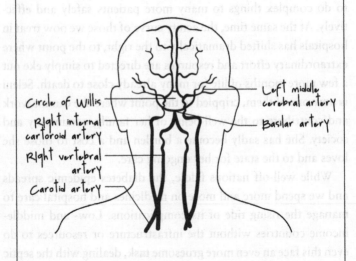

Medical revolutionaries–

we need more

IT WAS A LONG time ago that I was at med school at Otago although sometimes it seems I am not such a different person now to who I was then. I was a 'mature student' and perhaps more worldly than others but I was also unsure. I felt like I was from another world, already questioning why things were the way they were. I had been a student before. I had a degree from Victoria University in Wellington, rich in smatterings from Lloyd Geering's Comparative Religion class—I liked him. I liked the way he asked questions and thought for himself and I admired his courage in taking on the church through seeing the crucifixion of Christ in symbolic rather than literal terms. I took Classics too, featuring the fabulous sculptor Praxiteles famous for his languid S-curve seen in his magnificent statues—men so beautifully muscled and women with a real life softness and elegance— despite being sculpted from Carrara marble. At the opposite end of the spectrum were the stiff, freeze-dried, dead octopus, starfish and jellyfish of my Zoology class. Back then I had no idea what to do but I really enjoyed myself, gaining experience in living.

Then, still unclear of my future, together with other lost but intriguing souls I took up a job driving buses in Wellington. The buses were big and red, some diesel, the majority electric and all fun.

The induction programme for new drivers stretched over a six-week period. In my group was a bohemian ex-junkie, his literate girlfriend, a close friend from school and university, and me. Our instructor was a Yorkshire man who had a penchant for cream buns, especially the ones from the Seatoun cake shop.

Every day we would meet at the Courtenay Place depot, now a New World supermarket, for the bus-drivers' equivalent of the ICU morning huddle. A plan was made, the route to Seatoun decided, one of us allocated to drive, and off we went.

Once we reached Seatoun the huddle reconvened as we discussed road rules—we only gave way to concrete mixers—and common pitfalls that we might encounter in our new career.

The trolley buses were dangerous beasts—silent and lethal. At the command of your foot, surges of electricity descended down from the overhead wires, through those pesky poles, and into the heart of the beast. At first attempt, driving the trolley was like taming a wild horse—all raw power and scarily unpredictable. Slowly, with patience, practice and a soft foot, the power could be reined in.

The next challenge was how to change tracks, off the main line to another destination. Like trains pulling in and out of platforms at a station, trolley buses needed to do the same to get to where their passengers were waiting and, from there, to where the passengers wanted to go. That took some skill because changing tracks requires power to be applied as you cross the switch in the lines above. With power comes speed and with speed the embarrassment of your poles falling down. I say embarrassment because that was the prevailing sentiment among our group when our poles would drop—apart from at that well known spot at James Smith corner when all of us, at one time or another, deliberately brought our poles down changing from the number 3 to the number 2 route through the Mt Victoria bus tunnel. So notorious was this spot that if approached at exactly 15 kilometres per hour, not only would the poles come down but invariably one of the ropes holding them in place would break. A broken rope was a morning off and, from time to time, all of us needed one of those.

We wore a uniform; it was grey and made out of polyester. We ate often and badly, and we sat for long periods on red vinyl seats. At worst, it was a recipe for an early death. At best, the road to a bad case of haemorrhoids. I did it for a while but soon realised I couldn't keep driving buses forever.

More for fear of haemorrhoids than an early death, compounded by the profound sense of disappointment I felt in letting my father down, I started to look for an alternate career.

During my adolescence my father drove a series of flash cars, staring out as he did between the dashboard and steering wheel, his hat the one part of him visible to oncoming motorists. He never took public transport, nor did my mother, who rode in taxis when not with my father. What a surprise it was then when one morning at about 10.30 Dad made his way to the bus stop at the bottom of the Wadestown hill and waited for a ride home with his son. I was surprised and perhaps a little embarrassed because I knew what he thought of me doing this and not following a professional or academic career. He was really sweet and I think he enjoyed the ride and seeing me sitting up there. I suspect he was also a little reassured by the selection of books I had stacked up on the dash in front of me, perhaps thinking my choice right then was not necessarily wrong or a waste of time.

In those days there were many students in the same position as me. We'd all been to university and were looking around, wondering what to do and what career to follow—spending time in each other's company, solving the problems of the world and having a ball. That was a luxury and an investment enjoyed by many of my age including many of those now responsible for denying that same opportunity to the students of today. Who knows what might have happened to me if I had been forced into some other kind of employment or career before I was ready.

It was at an impromptu get-together that I met my fellow driver Jim. He was the son of a prominent physician from not far away. He really was the subject of his father's disappointment. We were in the depot. It was payday. The sun was shining down through the skylights, cutting hazy spotlights through the cigarette smoke onto the card players and conversationalists. I was at a table with Elias, on the run from the coup in Chile, Leota, the original laughing Samoan, and Jim, who had already been a bus driver for three years. Jim was smart and had been accepted to med school after his final year at school but he didn't know what to do so opted out for a bit. We laughed about 'a lifetime with haemorrhoids' and that's when he told me he'd decided to reapply for med school. It was then that I decided to do the same.

Without telling anyone, I got the papers, wrote my application, and started to get in the groove. I had an okay degree, although I'd never get a look-in these days. That said, I was reasonably confident that if I got an interview I might just swing it and persuade them to let me in. I put a lot of thought and time into my application, making much of the broader experiences that I'd had since leaving school. Strangely, it went as planned. I got the call, flew to Dunedin and enjoyed the interview.

The deep dashboard of my trolley bus was my bookcase. I was a big reader in those days and just before my med school interview I'd just finished reading *The Summing Up* by Somerset Maugham—it was a great read and of course I talked about it in my interview. I remember quoting a fabulous observation made about judges, 'I have wished that beside his bunch of flowers at the Old Bailey, his lordship had a packet of toilet paper. It would remind him that he was a man like any other.'

I was interested in the world and used to looking outwards. Once I got to med school, such were the workload and the hours, many students drifted away from real life and, despite explicit warnings from some of our professors, the gaze of many turned inwards. Down into the most fascinating of worlds, people tumbled, emerging periodically for air at a funeral, a wedding or occasionally at a good party.

I was single, still relatively young and discovering the potential of good conversation and charm in making new friends. I had a ball. Perhaps saved by my already well-entrenched bad habits, 'everything in moderation including excess', my gaze remained firmly outward.

I have never been a science type—50 per cent in School Certificate physics—nor am I particularly academic. I just scraped an A bursary and got an okay bachelor's degree. But when I hit med school I did really well. Maybe I was better balanced—I really don't know—but the work was fascinating and came easy, and I loved the people. I made lots of new friends, many from the corner bar at the Captain Cook where the emphasis was more on conversation than drinking. My friends there were artists, poets, lecturers from the English department and a steady stream of students like me who enjoyed a bit of excess in moderation.

Even back then I knew what mattered and what made the world go around— it was people. Throughout my career in medicine that hasn't changed. When I look for purpose in my work, it's about people and life. When I look for purpose in the provision of healthcare services, whether they be to an individual, a family or a population, nothing changes—it's also about people and life. I didn't learn that at med school, I learned it at the corner bar of the Captain Cook Tavern. Sadly, that is no more. There are new and more bankrupt lessons we are asking our young people to learn—the inherent value of many social services has been replaced by their cost and saleable value. Wind back the clock I say, remake the corner bar of the Captain Cook Tavern and bring back the conversation; send the grey men of government there for 10 years of reprogramming until they know full well the value of people and the sanctity of the world we live in.

I am no scholar of the history of medicine but I often think about what we do today and how that will be judged tomorrow. Looking back provides a degree of humility about what we understand and what more we have to learn. I see no end to that journey in the near future—we have evolved over many millions of years so to think otherwise smacks of arrogance. No matter where we are on that journey it is unlikely that our accumulation of knowledge will be matched by our ability to use it appropriately or even equitably. These are the skills that probably need researching, addressing and promoting more than scientific knowledge itself.

My friend Professor Sir Muir Gray is a Glaswegian public health doctor who lives in the English city of Oxford. He has a brain that is both big and agile, and I am a pupil of his in many ways. Although an intensivist, I am a public health doctor too. I know full well that the outcomes from what I do, so long as I do it well, are more determined by the patient than by me. Was the patient a rusty Skoda or a new Lexus before the disastrous crash? You get my drift.

These are concerns that many of us don't think about until how we have lived our lives catches up with us, physically and spiritually. I am not saying we need to obsess about every little thing but at least we can be a bit more sensible and not smoke, drink or eat ourselves to an early grave.

I care because I reckon if I met you I would like you. I care too because when it's you at death's door, it might be me in the middle of the night trying to get you working again. I care one more time because I am probably paying for your care and if I am paying for your care, someone else is missing out. That is still our world. Despite efforts by some to deny it, human beings in New Zealand are communal in their thinking, values, beliefs and behaviours, and long may that continue.

Like Muir Gray, I too am a revolutionary and see progress in modern medicine over the past 150 years through a revolutionary lens. We recognise the extraordinary events of 1854 London as emblematic of the first revolution in modern medicine. John Snow, a practising physician, became aware of and interested in an outbreak of disease causing diarrhoea, dehydration and subsequently death for many folk living in London—it was cholera.

Although not that long ago, the theories of disease in 1854 were very different from what they are now. Back then it was a commonly held belief that disease was caused and spread by bad air or 'miasma'. While many diseases are spread by things in the air, there was no knowledge then about what those things might be. There was no formal recognition or description of bacteria or viruses. Snow, now recognised as the world's first epidemiologist, meticulously identified all the cases of cholera. He recognised that all were associated with their close proximity to the Broad St pump in Soho. By disabling the pump by removing its handle, the epidemic was halted.

Later it was found that the Broad St water supply came from a well dug very close to an old sewer or cesspit from where the contamination arose. Snow's act to protect the public was emblematic of our first revolution in healthcare—the importance of public health.

Although traditionally the domain of public health practitioners, responsibility for interventions like this—recognising and providing clean water, immunisation, prevention of disease, stewardship of our environment—fall on all of us. As such, these are too important for us to allow them to be traded away by the grey-faced ideologues, hell bent on short-term gains.

Not long after, in 1890, at the request of sugar merchant and philanthropist Sir Henry Tate, Luke Fildes painted a now famous work called 'The Doctor'. It hangs in Tate's eponymous gallery in London. This is the description of the work written by Simon Wilson in *Tate Gallery: An Illustrated Companion*:

> In the final version of The Doctor, Fildes paints a young
> child in a rustic interior lying across two chairs, his pale
> face illuminated by the glass lamp on the table. The
> doctor, dressed in a tailored suit, sits beside the makeshift
> bed looking down at his patient anxiously. The boy's
> father, standing in the background with his hand on
> the shoulder of his wife whose hands are clasped as if
> in prayer, looks in to the grave face of the doctor. Their
> humble lifestyle is evident from the pewter, the scrap of
> carpet on the stone floor and their ragged clothing. The

extent of the youth's illness can be seen by the half empty medicine bottle on the table, and the bowl and jug, used to relieve the boy's temperature, on the bench. The bits of paper on the floor could be prescriptions made out by the doctor for medicine now already taken. Fildes described the shaft of daylight as signifying the imminent recovery of the child. He wrote: 'At the cottage window the dawn begins to steal in—the dawn that is the critical time of all deadly illnesses—and with it the parents again take hope into their hearts, the mother hiding her face to escape giving vent to her emotion, the father laying his hand on the shoulder of his wife in encouragement of the first glimmerings of the joy which is to follow.'[5]

This painting is rich in its imagery and has become a favourite for many in the profession, especially family doctors. In it there is so much about the relationship between the parties, the devotion of the doctor and, in particular, the anxiety and hope that is associated with someone becoming critically ill. This is made all the more poignant because the patient is a child.

'The Doctor' was painted well before the era of antibiotics, at a time when survival from infectious disease, particularly pneumonia, was in the lap of the gods. Back then the role of the physician was to offer symptomatic relief, prognostication and reassurance.

All that changed with the discovery of penicillin in 1928. Since then, we have witnessed a second revolution in healthcare—the rise of personal health services, characterised by the discovery of more pharmaceuticals and technologies to improve the quality and quantity of the lives of individual patients. This is perhaps best personified by the total hip joint replacement, voted by the

British Medical Journal as the operation of the twentieth century, perhaps because it is both so effective and ubiquitous.

Those personal health services include new generations of drugs that more effectively treat and cure people with cancer and a wide range of other previously crippling diseases like rheumatoid arthritis and other autoimmune diseases. These surgical and medical treatments are expensive but can be effective if used wisely. As a result, all countries are struggling to pay for them.

In New Zealand, although access to the newest medications might be delayed, the government drug buying agency Pharmac has kept the cost of pharmaceuticals down while improving access to most medications. Their bulk-buying approach, cost benefit analyses, and how they negotiate and trade with individual pharmaceutical firms is masterful. Despite their enormous profits, the shrinking cartel of increasingly wealthy and powerful drug companies continue to lobby governments around the world to disenfranchise Pharmac and prevent its approach spreading more widely. Their lobbying usually takes place on the quiet and behind the scenes, perhaps even on the golf courses of Hawai'i, but would probably have been most intense in the negotiations leading up to the recent signing of the Trans Pacific Partnership. Occasionally it can spill over into overt outrage and anger. This happened a few years ago at a meeting of the Commonwealth Fund—a private US foundation that is focused on providing a better healthcare system, especially for society's most vulnerable—in Washington. The then administrator of the Medicare and Medicaid services in the United States, Mark McClellan—brother of President George Bush's White House spokesman, Scott McClellan—launched an outright attack on New Zealand's approach to buying pharmaceuticals. This occurred at a dinner attended by our health minister, me as her advisor, and a small group of our best and brightest mid-career health practitioners and researchers who had been awarded Harkness Fellowships by the Commonwealth Fund.

In short, McClellan's argument was that countries like New Zealand were happy to reap the benefits of the investments made by drug companies but not pay the real costs. In that lies the core difference between how our two countries view health services—New Zealanders see them as a public good, while the United States view them as a series of profit-driven businesses. A little embarrassed by the brazen nature of this man's comments, we were unsure how to respond until, almost as one, we Kiwis began to hiss loudly while he droned on.

Whatever your position on this argument, we seem to have become victims of our own success with healthcare costs and affordability, now critical issues for all governments around the world.

That's not the only legacy of this explosion of knowledge and technology. We still have real and unsolved issues related to patient harm, waste, maximising value from what we spend our money on, health inequalities and inequities, and our ongoing failure to prevent disease.

Greater awareness of these problems towards the end of the last century brought on a third revolution in healthcare with the rise and rise of the quality improvement movement.

Up until that time, quality had been one of those mother-hood and apple pie terms—hard to define but usually something we recognise when it is either present or starkly absent in our interaction with the health services. As helpful as that might be, without a clearer definition of what we are talking about and appropriate measures to know if we are any good, quality of care is hard to improve.

From the 1990s, healthcare providers agreed on a definition of quality across a range of domains including safety and timelines; equality of access and equity of outcomes; and effectiveness of treatments and their cost effectiveness. This began the journey to better understand and meet the real needs and wants of patients.

Behind each of those domains lie a cascade of evidence-based actions and measures that were developed to improve patient care and in many places, Middlemore included, experts in improvement were specifically employed to help clinicians like me improve our performance.

Here is a recent example of a quality improvement initiative that has enhanced patient outcomes, reduced hospital costs and engaged clinical staff to do even more.

Patients in intensive care are extraordinarily vulnerable and at great risk of being harmed by the very people and interventions meant to help them. One of those risks is from a commonly occurring and potentially very dangerous blood stream infection associated with the use of large-bore intravenous catheters necessary to infuse drugs to treat patients with shock. Using an evidence-based set of interventions to standardise the insertion and maintenance of these lines, this infection has been largely eliminated. In New Zealand, this work was initiated by staff in my own intensive care unit at Middlemore Hospital then spread to all other ICUs in the country in an improvement effort led by Ko Awatea. As a result patient harm has been reduced and the estimated cost per infection of greater than NZ$20,000 saved. A secondary gain, and perhaps a more important one, was the engagement of clinical staff who have become enthused and more willing than ever before to embrace the ethos of 'we have two jobs, to do our job and to improve'. This resulted from the way this work was carried out, thereby fostering better team-work within intensive care units and allowing staff to find their own solutions to ensure reliability of their processes.

Although well established as 'business as usual' in many industries, especially those in the private sector, healthcare and many other areas of the public service have been slow to capitalise on this kind of progressive thinking. The reasons for this are complex but perhaps partially lie in a generalised lack of knowledge by health professionals about what's possible, absent leadership in this area, a lack of clarity about expectations and goals, little expertise in improvement and, most importantly, a belief that doctors know best.

By way of example consider the difference between subject matter expertise—being a doctor or a judge—and delivery expertise—providing a service that meets the quality standards discussed above. Clearly some doctors and judges will have these complementary skills but it is wrong to assume that just because I am a good intensive care doctor I can run a good intensive care service, let alone a hospital or a health service. In fact, many doctors are hopeless at this. In the same way, just because someone has been on the bench as a judge for 30 years does not mean that they can fix the problems of a system that they have been a part of for so long. As Albert Einstein said: 'We cannot solve our problems with the same thinking we used when we created them.'

Changing the way health services are planned and delivered requires a range of different and complementary skills, including those of doctors, people with improvement expertise, as well as patients and their families. There is also a place for production engineers to problem solve and improve the flow of people through our organisations. We also need experts from other industries to teach us about customer service and much more.

This kind of open thinking brings other benefits by challenging us to think more deeply about what we mean by 'health'. 'Health for what?' I commonly ask. Surely health for life, for being happy, for creating a sense of self-reliance, and for being productive as individuals, families and communities.

In the past the state and other healthcare funders obsessed about cost and volume. That view has changed to embrace quality and, more recently, the concept of value, defined simply as what we get for what we spend.

The practical application for this is called the 'Triple Aim'. It is made up of three key imperatives within the health system: managing costs and getting value for money; improving the quality of care and experience of care for individuals and families; and improving the overall health of our population.

Shifts in thinking like this are incredibly important. They open up the potential for new approaches to address debilitating legacy issues, and allow us to think about health through a broader lens in order to make more informed judgements about how policies in one area might affect another. A simple example of that is the impact of housing policy on the health of children.

As a result, while still acknowledging the value of important individual programmes like immunisation and vaccination, we can redefine population health more broadly to also consider the impact of climate change, housing, levels of employment and the minimum wage, our diet and more on our health and who we want to be as individuals and a nation.

Inconveniently complex, you might say. Yes, you're right, but at least it's real! Only when we embrace this complexity and the interdependence of so many factors necessary to produce the outcomes we want will we actually have a show of getting there. There is a term used for this kind of thinking—it's called transformation, a word many find easy to say but difficult to action. To date there has been little official interest in dealing with the root causes of the complex mix of issues bleeding our social services dry. But as I sit here there are signs that the conversation might be changing, with some asking for help and quietly speaking to those who know better.

When I was young and handsome, I fell in love with a fabulous woman, not just because she was beautiful but because she was smart, funny and in her own unique way amusingly quirky. We first met over an orange. She was peeling it carefully with a knife and managed to skin the whole thing such that the entire peel came off in one piece. I thought that was impressive but more was to come. She then spent a lot of time meticulously peeling the pith from around the skinned orange before separating out the individual segments then, piece by piece, we ate it. When I asked about her technique, especially the care she took in removing the pith, she replied, 'Don't you know? If you eat the pith, it layers around your heart.'

'From a medical family?' I asked.

There is a lovely naivety and innocence about this. Whether or not her belief has changed, she continues to do it the same way today.

In its own way, modern medicine is a belief system too but one based on the scientific method or at the very least cumulative anecdote and expert opinion. Crucially, though, it must be open to scrutiny and review. Like other belief systems modern medicine has its own creation story, history and tradition. One book of that gospel, the birth of modern anaesthesia, now elevated to biblical status in the minds of all anaesthetists, is permanently etched on my brain. Here is a snippet:

The father of modern anaesthesia is credited as
W.T.G Morton who gave ether to a patient in Boston,
Massachusetts in October 1846.

Prior to this, techniques for anaesthesia included,
alcohol, opium, cannabis and hypnosis. Nitrous oxide
(laughing gas) was first used in 1844 by Horace Wells.

Before anaesthesia was introduced surgery was a last
resort and operations able to be performed were few.
Most patients were held down, or if lucky, fainted.
Many died.

Anaesthesia developed rapidly with the introduction of
many new and safer drugs, allowing come complex and
longer operations.

Professor James Young Simpson introduced chloroform
in 1847 and this was given successfully to Queen
Victoria by John Snow for the birth of Prince
Leopold . . .

And so it goes.

Other cultures have different belief systems to cure and to heal
that are as influential in those places as modern medicine is in the
west. Take Samoa, for example—a small, proud, independent
nation in the middle of the Pacific Ocean, where a largely homog-
enous population has lived for over three thousand years. The
Samoan people have a powerful, impressive and deeply rooted
set of values and beliefs. Central in that is the place of traditional
healers, while the impact and reach of western medicine remains

limited because of a lack of accessible primary care, poorly developed systems and limited local capabilities.

At the age of seventeen, Tina gave birth to her first child whom she breastfed. When the baby was two weeks old, Tina had a minor breast infection that was treated with the application of leaves by a local healer. Tina's breast got better quite quickly but she didn't. Over the next six weeks she became increasingly tired, had sweats, backache and recurrent fevers. During this time, she consulted three other healers and saw a traditional massage therapist twice a week.

One morning she woke with a painful dusky blue foot. She was treated for this with more traditional medicines and massage. Another two weeks later, at death's door, she arrived at the hospital. Tina was lethargic and feverish, struggling with her breathing and with signs of heart and kidney failure.

Examining her more closely, she had the classic findings of advanced infective bacterial endocarditis, a bacterial infection of the heart valves. Her symptoms included finger clubbing, a strange deformity that leaves the finger tips looking like the end of drumsticks; splinter haemorrhages, tiny blood clots that run vertically under the nails; small haemorrhages in the conjunctivae of her eyes; and, most obviously, a cold black leg that was now clearly gangrenous. Listening to her heart, she had a raging murmur consistent with a leaky mitral valve.

A cardiac echo confirmed the problem and identified a massive 10-millimetre infected clot, adherent to the posterior leaflet of her mitral valve. We could see it flapping backwards and forward with each beat of Tina's heart, and with each beat the chances of more infected debris dislodging and flying off increased. Already some had lodged in her fingernails, others were in her eyes, and a bigger one was blocking the blood flow in her leg. The echo also showed that Tina had thickened abnormal heart valves caused by undiagnosed rheumatic heart disease. This explained why she had become so ill following such a minor infection in the first place. What a tragedy. If she had been diagnosed and then treated with the monthly penicillin injections that kept so many others like her safe, she would now be well and at home with her baby. Instead, here she was needing an above-knee amputation of her leg. Then, if she survived that, her life would only be saved by an operation to replace her mitral valve.

That became impossible. The next day, her left leg now gone and her place on a theatre list in an Auckland hospital four hours' flight away assured, debris from that huge clot on her mitral valve worked itself loose. Carried at pace through the left ventricle and out through the aortic valve into the aorta, like a pooh stick in a river, it followed the current up into her carotid artery and from there into her left middle cerebral artery where it became stuck, effectively blocking blood flow to the entire left hemisphere of her brain. A similar pooh stick took another route into the left vertebral artery to block the posterior inferior cerebellar artery, knocking off a large part of the posterior part of her brain. These things just happened—there was no song and dance, no obvious signal. It was just that she didn't wake up in the ICU and, although moving abnormally to a painful stimulus applied to her left hand and foot, she had no motor response to a painful stimulus on the right side of her body.

Later that morning, we scanned her brain and saw it—the dark areas of cerebral infarction or stroke in the territories of those vessels now blocked. Strokes often leave focal deficits causing a spastic paralysis or weakness of parts of the body—typically a weakness or paralysis of one arm and leg—but if large territories of the brain lose blood supply the swelling that accompanies these catastrophes can cause damage from which there is a loss of consciousness and no realistic hope of recovery. Sadly this was the case for Tina, so later that day we removed her from the ventilator and she died several hours later surrounded by her family.

Saving young Tina's life would have happened if her rheumatic fever had been diagnosed. Saving young Tina's life would have happened if the traditional healers and modern medical practitioners had more respect for each other, and she had been seen at the hospital earlier. Saving Tina's young life was totally possible but just didn't happen because things are the way they are. Sadly, in that place there are many Tinas and there will be more until these fundamental issues are addressed.

Despite mature health systems in the better resourced nations of the world, strongly held belief systems like the one just described abound there too. A few years ago much of the world was affected and terrified by an outbreak of a swine flu virus for which there was no specific treatment apart from symptom control and organ support. Historians and experts in the field remembered the devastating effects of the influenza epidemic of 1919, estimated to have killed between 50 and 100 million people worldwide, including one quarter of the population of Samoa much to the shame of the New Zealand administration at the time.

The young, the elderly and pregnant women seemed most vulnerable to this latest strain of flu but clearly many others became ill too. One of those was a farmer from the Waikato. So ill did he become that he ended up on an extra corporeal membrane oxygen machine to do the work of his failing lungs as well as needing renal dialysis to temporise for his failed kidneys. Believe me, no one gets sicker than this. In the end Alan survived—to some it was thanks to a miracle from G-d, to others it was because of exceptionally good care, and to some it was all put down to the high doses of intravenous vitamin C he received at the behest of his family. His case became a cause célèbre for the vitamin C lobby—yes, there is one—and he became the subject of a *60 Minutes* documentary. This clip is available on YouTube, accompanied by this introduction written by the proponents of vitamin C:

> Doctors treating Auckland farmer Alan Smith had
> decided it was time to turn his life support machine off,
> until a timely intervention by his family and vitamin C
> saved his life.

A simple google search of vitamin C will reveal a foundation established to promote its efficacy in all things including (but not restricted to) curing cancer and being an antidote to all known toxins. The same foundation diss the use of conventional treatments for many life-threatening conditions which they are convinced vitamin C alone will assuredly cure. Following the publicity about Alan's case, it was no surprise that the families of other patients with swine flu in our ICUs began to demand the same treatment. Medical staff around the country, supported by their peer group, the College of Intensive Care Medicine, resolutely refused. As a result, battlelines were drawn and the parties were at war.

I too appeared in that *60 Minutes* documentary, I suspect portrayed as a demonic unbeliever in the eyes of some. Cheekily, I was sceptical of the cause and effect relationship between Alan receiving vitamin C and his eventual recovery. We have very few magic bullets in medicine and I simply cannot accept that we had one there. For their part, the vitamin C lobby cannot believe that I cannot believe. Some of them went further to say that proponents of western medicine like me are peddling deceit and corruption.

I know only too well that modern medicine does not hold a monopoly on the truth nor does it have explanations for many of the mysteries we witness in everyday life—even though some in my profession might pretend it does. Perhaps it's partly because of this, and the patronising approach of many modern medical practitioners toward their patients in general, that huge swathes of society believe in and take advantage of alternative and complementary treatments.

In fact, when families ask me whether they can bring complementary medicines into the ICU, so long as I am satisfied that they won't cause harm, I usually say yes because I define benefit more broadly. Although there is little to no evidence of improvement from most of these treatments, if they allow the family to feel as though they are actively contributing to their loved one's care and that promotes a sense of trust in me and what my team are doing, I see a benefit to their use.

That was not the case here though. While there is a small potential for harm to the critically ill when high-dose vitamin C is given intravenously, my main objection to its use was because of how the vitamin C lobby groups responded in the case of Alan Smith by attributing all benefit—even his survival—to it alone. They then use that to actively promote vitamin C as a universal cure-all when clearly there is no credible evidence for this. On the face of it, its proponents seem remarkably similar to the snake-oil salespeople of the 1800s preying on the desperate and, in so doing, promising false hope and it is this behaviour that I find so unacceptable. When we are doing our best to help the critically ill, there may well be a place for some traditional and complementary forms of treatment but there is no place for outright dishonesty.

Whatever your beliefs, these are unhelpful spats that should be overcome as we embrace the changes of the latest (and most welcome) of revolutions in healthcare—the revolution of people and of knowledge, of co-design, morality and respect.

Modern medicine, reluctant or not, will be forced to mature to a point where it can acknowledge that it does not have all the answers on its own and never will. Increasingly we are seeing healthcare professionals, organisations and whole health systems less interested in foisting treatments on people without a better understanding of what they value. They are also actively seeking to engage with their communities to redesign the services that were always supposed to be for the benefit of the people. Using the resources and power within teams and across organisations and social services to deliver meaningful outcomes for individuals, families and communities has the promise to radically change the equation such that one plus one might equal five or ten, but never just two.

New Zealand's Alcohol and Other Drug Treatment Courts (AODTC) are an example of this kind of transformational thinking in action. Begun by a small group of judges, including my wife Ema, to address recidivist criminal offending which is fuelled by drug and alcohol addiction, it is a model of the kind of cooperation across multiple services that is increasingly necessary to address the real life problems that we have struggled with for ages.

Based on an American model and championed by the National Association of Drug Court Professionals (NADCP), the AODTC have an evidence base for success that is formidable.

In New Zealand, more than 80 per cent of all offences are committed under the influence of alcohol or drugs, and the cost of incarceration for one year is close to NZ$100,000. A significant number of prisoners reoffend due to a variety of issues, including drug and alcohol dependence, against a background of challenging social circumstances.

Our traditional approach to punishment has been to fine and imprison offenders but you cannot punish away addiction. The folly of that approach has now been accepted and a new approach, based on successful models in other jurisdictions, is being piloted in the Auckland and Waitakere district courts in New Zealand.

The programme is over halfway through its five-year pilot scheme dealing with high-risk, high-needs offenders, and from early on results are impressive. Reported back in July 2013, in the two years prior to entering the court, this cohort of offenders committed 900 offences. In the twelve months since entering the court, this number has dropped to only eleven.

Participants in the court are referred by lawyers and judges, and their acceptance into the court is predicated on them accepting responsibility for their offending, pleading guilty to their charges, and making a contractual commitment to abide by the rules of the court.

The intervention is a multidisciplinary one led by individual judges. The teams comprise of a judge, case managers, a court coordinator, a pou oranga (Māori cultural advisor), defence lawyers, police prosecutors, and peer support workers. The case manager works with others to identify the appropriate treatment for the individual, and liaises closely with the various providers.

Instead of taking up their usual adversarial roles, defence and prosecution lawyers and the other team members work to the same purpose: keeping the offender in treatment and drug and alcohol free; ensuring that the offender addresses other significant rehabilitative issues and does not reoffend; and ultimately to restore them to a productive life with a driver's licence and a job.

Each sitting day, all of the AODTC team meet together in closed court to go through the issues for each of the participants before seeing them in open court later in the day. Despite being in open court, these appearances are like nothing else within the justice system—intimate, very personal, deeply challenging and exceptionally moving.

In New Zealand, one of the objectives in providing this alternative to imprisonment is to address the gross over-representation of Māori in the imprisoned population, with over half of the participants in the AODTC being Māori. Further, the court appears to be developing its own tikanga—or cultural practices—which has been greatly enhanced by the role of pou oranga. This can be seen in the opening and closing of the court and in the graduation ceremony.

Tikanga can be described as general behavioural guidelines for daily life and interaction in Māori culture. Tikanga is commonly based on experience and learning that has been handed down through generations. It is also based on logic and common sense associated with a Māori world view.

The principles that underpin tikanga-based practices are personal and can have a relevance to people from all cultures and therefore to all drug court participants.

As a result of the court's interventions its participants can make and sustain meaningful and pro-social changes in their lives. They are also able to rediscover the simple kind of happiness and joy that comes with ordinary life experiences without the need for alcohol or drugs.

Alcohol and drug addiction is a chronic disease and the approach taken by the AODTC is perhaps the most effective chronic disease management model I know of. How ironic that it should have come from the judiciary rather than from the health system. This is the face of success and this is the looking glass we need to step through to help many people with other long-term conditions help themselves.

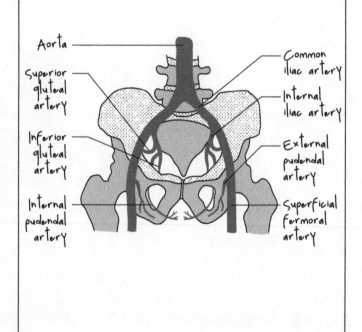

the Pelvic Arteries

CHAPTER 6

Close calls—

the thin line between life and death

MY CHILDREN AND MORE recent friends see me as they do in the here and now. Old friends, especially those I have known for many years, see me in a different light. Not always as the middle-aged man that I have become but me as I was through the time of our friendship, in my early days as the fat child who was always hungry and constantly begging the neighbours for more food; later as the talented young tennis player sliding into a low backhand volley on the grass courts at Wellington's Central Park or White City in London or as the first XV fullback in his first ever game of serious rugby, fending off the brutes from the Tawa under-nineteen team to score a try in the corner; or maybe as the embarrassed first XI cricketer, distracted by the sight of a pair of ferric-oxide coloured socks worn by Willy Simpson's father on the terraces at Wellington College and being clean bowled for a duck in the do-or-die annual match with Palmerston North Boys' High School. Well, that's what I hope.

These are just a few of the moments in time that have stuck with me. Of course, there are many others, all inexplicable combinations of circumstance, good luck and bad, and perhaps fate where things could have gone either way—that chance meeting in the med school café with a stranger leads to talk about a girl and before you know it, I have been with her for 34 years; the conversation with Jim, the bus driver, and me here now, a doctor of many years; my cousin Denis, a young man, through no fault of his own was in the wrong place at the wrong time and, in an instant, dead forever since 1978. These accidents in life, good and bad, seem as random as can be and fill me with equal quantities of wonder and dread at how they came about, and what might have been if they had not happened at all.

More often though what we get is the result of the choices we make. Why we make those choices is sometimes obvious, sometimes not. As an intensive care doctor, I make hundreds of decisions a day, a good number of which are obvious, rational, and based on a form of explicit knowledge and a strong body of evidence. However, many decisions come from another place, a kind of tacit knowledge gained from experience that may never reach the level of proof to become evidence. Almost always, those decisions are reinforced by an intuitive element, a kind of sixth sense or gut instinct that this is the right thing to do.

When things are most critical and an immediate course of action is called for, usually there's no explicit knowledge to guide me, and in that unique moment of time, no shared tacit knowledge that I can reliably trust. Instead, there's a powerful sense of knowing what to do, right there and then. This gut feeling or sixth sense plays out in ways that I can feel and almost taste. When it comes, it is a feeling that I now recognise and trust—and ignore at my peril.

Carlos lived in the eastern suburbs of the city in a house that looked modern and Mediterranean. In the backyard was a terrific swimming pool. There were similar houses all around, separated by good-sized gardens and wide streets, all under a big sky. Even on still days you could smell the sea only a few hundred metres away down the hill.

Carlos was fifty, long married with four kids and a dog. He was born in a far-off land and came here as a single man seeking adventure and good fortune. On all fronts he had succeeded. Soon after arriving he landed a job with a construction firm and, through determination and hard work, he became foreman then manager and, eventually, the owner of the company. Carlos loved to swim and cycle and had always been an extremely fit guy, preferring physical activity to watching television and drinking beer. His kids called him OCD and perhaps he was, choosing to sublimate that potentially destructive tendency into things much more socially acceptable, like his work and his fitness.

Like many cyclists, he had smooth bulging calf muscles, matched only by the smoothness of his head and his manner. He ran his business well, like clockwork, paying attention to detail in the very best of ways. His employees loved him and said that he had a big heart made of gold.

Sandy, his wife, relied on him for all things. She was capable and smart, but it was Carlos that made the decisions, and it was Carlos around whom the activities of the house were largely centred. Don't take this the wrong way—this was just the way it was; it worked and their house was a happy house. All that changed one sunny Friday evening.

I was the on-call intensive care specialist in my hospital. It had been a slow day. I was thinking about going home and leaving things to the registrars when my phone went off, signalling a trauma call and requesting my presence in the emergency department.

Somewhere out there in the real world, right now, on a road, in a house, something bad is happening. Someone is in real trouble and at risk of dying. An ambulance has been called—there are tears, grief, anxious relatives or bystanders. It might be a crash scene with people already dead—the street littered with broken glass and personal effects. It could be a child run over in a driveway. Whatever the scene, no matter if there's chaos or outright danger, paramedics will be sent into it willingly. Cool, well-trained and confident, they will make a rapid assessment of what they find, call for help if they need to, and calm the situation. At the same time, they will fall into their practised approach to stabilise the patient as best they can and, depending on the nature of the patient's condition and the proximity of the nearest hospital, they might do a scoop and run—load the patient and leave immediately. In all cases of serious and life-threatening injury or illness, they will call ahead to forewarn the hospital that they are coming. These calls are then relayed to the appropriate medical staff, who assemble in the emergency department or ambulance bay to meet the crew, hear the story, and get to work on the patient.

On this occasion the 111 call was from a rural back road that ran between orchards and horse paddocks in the south of the city. It was a relatively orderly scene—a few cars stopped on the side of the road and a big SUV parked at an angle, stopping traffic from going through. Just beyond that, a group of motorists were gathered alongside an unconscious man dressed in Lycra, his broken bicycle in a ditch 40 metres back.

Realising the gravity of the situation, the paramedics quickly put an oxygen mask on the man's face, stabilised his neck in a stiff collar, and carefully clipped a scoop stretcher underneath him. They loaded him into the ambulance, called ahead and sped for the nearest trauma hospital.

Despite practising for scenarios like this, and becoming slick in managing them, these are always tense times. While waiting for the ambulance to arrive, we assembled in one of the resuscitation rooms to organise ourselves—a critically injured cyclist, unconscious, likely shocked from blood loss and close to death.

I was appointed team leader to oversee the immediate management. An emergency department doc and a senior nurse would assess and manage the patient's airway and breathing. The surgical doc, another ED doc and a nurse were allocated to assess and manage the patient's circulation, insert two large bore drips for fluid resuscitation, and be responsible for giving all the medications to the patient as required. Finally, a senior nurse was assigned to be our scribe, to record everything that we did and when we did it.

We heard the ambulance before we could see it, its siren blaring loudly all the way to the ambulance bay. On arrival, the patient was breathing oxygen delivered by a standard mask. As we transferred him onto the resus room trolley, one of the paramedics gave us the handover.

The patient was an as-yet unidentified male of about fifty. A woman on her way home from work had found him sprawled on the road. She rushed to help and called 111. A few minutes later an ambulance arrived. The man was unconscious, with a large gash over his right eye, its pupil appearing dilated and not reacting to light, as it should. He was breathing but had a very fast and thready pulse and a blood pressure so low we couldn't even measure it. He had multiple abrasions and small cuts everywhere, as well as skin loss in several places where he had skidded along the road.

Later another witness came forward with a more detailed story. The man had been cycling when a truck and trailer unit overtook him at about 80 to 100 kilometres per hour. He saw that the left stabilising arm of the trailer was unsecured and it was this that struck the man from behind, hitting him across his lower back, catapulting him through the air and onto the road. The truck did not stop and was long gone by the time the first passer-by arrived.

It was pretty obvious from the outset that he was as close to dying as it gets, most likely from internal bleeding. He was deeply unconscious and that fixed and dilated right pupil suggested a severe, usually fatal, underlying brain injury. He was barely breathing but despite that had good air entry into both lungs. We could not feel an actual pulse though he had a pulse rate on the monitor of 170 beats per minute and he was ice-cold to touch.

We quickly intubated him to take over his breathing. As we did this, almost imperceptibly, I saw him move his left arm in a way that should not happen if he'd had as serious a brain injury as the pupillary sign suggested. My colleagues inserted a couple more lines to take bloods and give him fluids and we quickly went over him to narrow down his source of blood loss.

There are only a few places blood can go in a scenario like this: on the floor, but there was no torrential external bleeding to cause this degree of shock; into the long bones associated with fractures, but there were none; into the chest, but again there was no sign of that when we listened to his breath sounds and his chest X-ray was clear; into the belly, which was a real possibility here, but at that time, we didn't have the portable ultrasound technology available to rule that out, so we remained suspicious; the final injury that can cause this degree of exsanguination is from a severely fractured pelvis with blood lost into the tissues of the posterior abdominal wall or retroperitoneum. This had to be the place because it was obvious that his pelvis was completely shattered. Quickly, we wound a sheet around him to stabilise his pelvis, called the interventional radiologist to come in to help us, then we raced up to the operating theatres. My plan was to get the surgeons to open his belly, deal with any haemorrhage there or reassure us that he was not bleeding into the abdomen while waiting for the interventional radiologist to do his magic and stop the pelvic bleeding.

Twenty-five minutes after arriving in the ED, we were in the operating room. The on-call surgeon was not terribly enthusiastic, citing the fixed and dilated pupil, the degree of shock, and the rate of ongoing haemorrhage as reasons why this man wouldn't survive. He suggested instead that we make him comfortable and wait for what he believed would be his inevitable death. I quickly countered his arguments—the abnormal pupil was most likely the result of a direct injury to the eye, not the brain. He was a young and fit-looking man. And I had a strong gut feeling we should press on!

In emergencies like this, doctors follow a set guideline to rapidly assess and manage life-threatening situations. It's called the ABCD approach—airway, breathing, circulation and disability or level of consciousness. In the trauma setting, we call this the primary survey and it is designed to deal with immediate threats to a person's life. Once completed, we then begin the secondary survey—a comprehensive head-to-toe examination of the patient followed by appropriate investigations: blood tests, X-rays and CT scans. In this case we were stuck at C—we needed to stop the bleeding as soon as possible.

As soon as the surgeon opened his belly it became clear that there was no intra-abdominal bleeding but, instead, ongoing torrential haemorrhage into the retroperitoneum, as we suspected. We could actually see it, the tissues there bulging and blistering before our eyes—it was a sight I will never forget. If anything looked 'fatal', this was it. Pelvic bleeding can be like a rupture in a reservoir: blood pours out like water down a water-fall. Damaged by the sideways shearing of the pelvic bones, the big arteries and veins—the ones that ferry blood to and from the lower half of the body—shear and empty their contents into the tissues as fast as the flow of blood to them.

There are only a few effective treatments for this kind of injury. Certainly stabilising the pelvis with a sheet can help as a first-aid measure, but once in hospital, torrential bleeding of this sort is best stopped by our radiology colleagues, sometimes helped by external fixation of the pelvis by the orthopaedic surgeons. The radiologists use X-ray technology to guide small catheters into the distal vessels deep inside the body and inject a radio-opaque dye into them to identify the bleeding points. Once identified, they then inject small amounts of Gelfoam and coils of wire into those vessels to effectively stop the bleeding. It sounds crude and it is. It sounds easy but it isn't. Who said a childhood spent on the Xbox is wasted? It's exactly those skills that are needed to twist and guide these fine catheters along the vessels and round tight corners to places that surgeons' hands will never reach without causing more harm than good.

It was clear that our mystery man was losing blood faster than we could replace it and his blood pressure was still danger-ously low. The combined effect of prolonged hypotension, and the torrential and ongoing bleeding into his retroperitoneum, effectively obliterated the normal pressure gradients in the kidney necessary to make urine, causing his kidneys to fail. This was no surprise, but it meant more than ever that time was of the essence. The more he bled, the more blood we needed to give him. If only it was as simple as replacing what is lost, but it's not. This kind of loss and replacement has consequences of its own.

As all of this was swirling through my mind, I told the surgeon to clamp the patient's aorta, just above where it divides to become the left and right common iliac arteries. By doing this for a short period, I hoped we might be able to stem the blood loss while we waited for the radiologist. It seemed like an age, all this waiting, but in real time it was no more than twenty minutes. We were pouring in blood, platelets, clotting factors, giving calcium, running noradrenaline through a long line in the neck, sending bloods to the lab; receiving the results, all looking increasingly ugly, so in our minds we were preparing for the worst.

I was so relieved to see the radiologist arrive and thrilled that it was Rowshan. He grew up in Iran and had lived through extraordinary times—he was my friend and he was an absolute master of his trade.

As he got to work, I kept my eye on the monitors, especially the cardiac trace (ECG). All patients will die if you cannot stop this kind of bleeding; continually replacing blood in an ongoing fashion is never enough. Massive blood loss like this causes a raft of metabolic problems as a result of poor tissue perfusion, and the need for ongoing transfusion compounds that, especially because of an increasing potassium and acid load that cannot be excreted because of the renal failure. As the potassium rises, muscles lose their ability to effectively contract, and the muscle that matters most here is the heart. High potassium changes the normal narrow complex of the ECG trace making it increasingly broad so, like a drunk, slowing and slurring, it too will eventually stop.

Rowshan did well, stopping the bleeding one vessel at a time, and my crew were replacing what we could, all the while treating the complications of all of that. Despite all of that good work, time was passing and his bloods were becoming increasingly abnormal but unusually, this man's ECG trace stayed resolute as it articulately and reliably made its way across screen after screen, beep after beep.

Something unusual was going on here. It had started in the emergency department with that flick of his hand and continued in the operating theatre. I had been here before—in situations with much less bleeding than this, with bloods not half as bad as these were—and in each case it had ended badly. No sign of that here. This man, whoever he was, was made of tough stuff.

Over the next few hours, we did all we could to control his increasingly abnormal metabolism using infusions of bicarbonate to balance the accumulating acids in his blood, boluses of intravenous calcium, glucose and insulin to lower his potassium level and before I knew it our evening had turned into night and suddenly it was 1 a.m. on Saturday morning.

With most of the bleeding now controlled, we prepared to move our patient across the corridor to the ICU. By then, we had given him 65 units of blood products and over 30 litres of other fluids—over ten times the normal volume of blood in his body. This was a huge transfusion, but most of that came out into the tissues of the retroperitoneum. Miraculously, he was still alive.

Our mystery man was still on a ventilator, I hoped asleep as a result of the sedation we were giving him rather than unconscious due to a massive head injury. What I did know was that he was far too unstable for us to move him to be scanned in order to find out one way or the other. As it was, we were still only partway through our guideline for the assessment and management of severe trauma and still stuck at C!

Just keeping him alive had been our focus. He had multiple lines in now—big intravenous catheters in his right and left internal jugular veins for fluids, drugs and dialysis; an arterial line in the radial artery of his wrist; the large bore sheath in the right femoral artery through which Rowshan had so skilfully directed his catheters; a nasogastric tube to drain his stomach; his breathing tube of course attached to a $65,000 ventilator; and a urinary catheter, its drainage bag sadly empty of urine.

Although some of his bloods tests were better, because his kidneys had failed his blood desperately needed cleaning up. Gingerly, we got him onto dialysis with small boluses of adrenaline to keep his blood pressure up.

It had been a weird evening and I was sure something unusual and mysterious was afoot. I was exhausted but energised and strangely elated too! I walked around the ICU, checked on the other patients and then took a stroll outside. It was a beautiful night. In days past, I would have jumped the fence and gone for a swim in the hospital pool, but that was now long gone. I was hungry but all that was available was crap from an array of vending machines better trained to take your money than give you sustenance. A comfortable chair and my feet up on a verandah rail looking out across the night sky would have done but there was nowhere for that. Sitting in an office looking out the window wasn't even possible because there were no offices with windows available to me. How weird, I thought, this place is supposed to make people better but it is so awful on so many counts.

There was one saving grace though: hospitals at night, stranger places than they are during the day, are ripe for the imagination to flourish. Like the southern motorway at the same dead time of night, they too have one long, empty corridor after another.

The only signs of life are an occasional cleaner in a cowboy hat riding a big floor polisher, our equivalent of a growling road-working machine lit up like a Christmas tree. Like the odd car, an occasional house surgeon will run a red between well-lit pods that could be gas stations but instead are the nursing stations on the wards. I want to breathalyse them all.

'Life can only be understood backwards, but it must be lived forwards,' said the great Danish philosopher Søren Kierkegaard. Ghosts and memories flood back to you in those dark hours before the dawn. Did Mama, the thirteen-year-old girl from Aitutaki, really need to die? Couldn't we have done more? Dr Ken Mayo, his photo on the wall at the entrance to the radiology department, dead at fifty. His weathered face above his Viyella shirt and neatly knotted tie etched in my brain forever. I never want to end like that, all alone, dropping dead at work. I used to worry that one day I too would be remembered by a photo on a wall in the ICU but as time has passed so too has my anxiety about ending that way, certainly at that age.

I carried on past the entrance to the closed cafeteria and remembered the time I organised a concert by Tim Finn, who played to a crowd of kids and adults, all with burn injuries. The venue was grungy, the ceiling suitably low and pockmarked, much like the one at Ronnie Scott's club in Soho. It was 25 June, Tim's birthday and, at the end, all the patients and staff returned the favour and sang him a rousing version of 'Happy Birthday'. He said it was the best present he'd ever had, and both he and I almost cried.

Down towards the coronary care unit I drifted. This place was a good run from the ICU on the first floor of the Galbraith block, opposite the Middlemore railway station. I've lost count of the number of long sprints I've done from one end of the hospital to the other to rescue patients from their hearts stopping prematurely, at the same time always anxious they might restart long after damage to the brain is certain. Arriving there, gasping, I would wonder whether I was next in line for a coronary. Catching my breath, I would follow the ACLS guidelines to shock and thump that dumb organ back into sinus rhythm.

At the end of each case, no matter the result, we always had an informal debrief over a cup of tea and a gingernut—biscuits that were always present in the jar at the nurses' station. Looking back, these were special times: our performance was reviewed, new relationships were formed, and old ones reaffirmed.

As I wandered, I remembered the day in the early 1990s when—after a long and unsuccessful attempt to resuscitate a youngish man—we found the cookie jar empty and the tea no longer available. There was no debrief that day and we all trudged disconsolate back to our home wards. Soon after, the crackers, cheese and jam disappeared from the theatre tearoom, and with that stopped the unspoken, easy and relaxed conviviality that resulted from those of us attracted to it.

A face seen is a problem solved but there seemed little time or place for that kind of simple interaction between members of the specialist staff so soon after the mother of all budgets. More from less was the philosophy of the day. The buildings became meaner, the spaces smaller, access to the outdoors and natural light were not valued then nor are they much now. These are not environments conducive to learning, building and sustaining working relationships. They are places that I do my best to avoid and, when at all possible, leave.

Not long after that calamity, the hospital swimming pool—the closest world away from the turmoil and drama of the ICU and the wards you could ever imagine—was closed. Within a week it was covered with concrete. They certainly can be efficient when they want to!

Eventually, I went back to the ICU; it was close to 4 a.m. There I met Sandy and some of her family. She had become anxious when her husband of thirty years had not returned home from his bike ride so began looking for him, eventually phoning Middlemore. She was distraught when they told her that someone fitting his description was a patient in our hospital. Not knowing whether this was her husband, she told me things about him that I recognised. She then burst into tears when I gave her the medallion he had been wearing around his neck. A short while later, we went in to see him and then returned to the privacy of another room to talk.

Over the next little while I learned more about this man who was refusing to die. He was a family man with four children, and he ran a small successful business. When he was young he was a member of the Parachute Regiment of the British Army and had been a fitness fanatic ever since. Yesterday, he had been out training in preparation for a triathlon later in the year. Sandy described him as a dynamo, determined, committed and when he needed to be, totally focused on the task ahead. As she was speaking I could feel myself nodding in agreement as though I knew him almost as well as her.

Back in the ICU, the man I now knew to be Carlos had been remarkably stable but at five in the morning, his pulse rate steadily climbed and his blood pressure began to sag. He was bleeding again. Back came Rowshan and this time, with the help of a portable radiology machine, he slid his catheter back into that sheath in the femoral artery, painstakingly sought out the bleeding vessels and once again dealt with them one at a time.

By the time he had finished, the sun was up and we had burned through another 30 units of blood products.

Carlos needed more dialysis before things calmed down, and then at 10 a.m. on Saturday, we finally took him to the CT suite to finish our assessment of his injuries. Just as I thought—no brain injury; chest clear; no damage to internal organs in the abdomen; several fractures of his lumbar spine without much displacement of the bones; a totally destroyed pelvis; and massive soft-tissue swelling, extending from the lower back to his thighs.

By this stage too, both his calves had become tense and swollen, and his feet cool and pulseless. We call this the 'compartment syndrome' and it is the result of a number of factors that effectively stop the blood flow to the muscles and tissues of a limb. Here in Carlos that was most likely a result of all the fiddling with the vessels in his pelvis, the massive transfusion needed to keep him alive, and the pressure of blood in the tissues of his back and thighs. Once recognised, our surgeons quickly opened the skin and the fascia of his lower legs, dropping the pressure in those muscle compartments, and thereby restoring their blood supply. Once that had been done, I finally went home to bed.

Carlos spent three months in the ICU. During that time, he had a series of complications and setbacks that almost took his life. After multiple bouts of infection, he was finally discharged to the ward, a skeleton of a man, his face badly scarred and blind in one eye. Most of the muscle in his buttocks was gone, a side-effect of the intervention to stop the bleeding on that first night. The same shearing forces in his pelvis that ruptured his arteries and veins, together with the enormous pressure in the soft tissues around those shattered bones, also crushed many of the important nerves to his legs so Carlos could not stand or walk. These devastating physical injuries kept him in hospital for many weeks, followed by months in the spinal unit before he finally went home.

Carlos' life was changed forever, but he says he is grateful to me for saving his life. We see each other from time to time, at least once a year for lunch. There have been many lunches now and, during that time, he and his family have been through so much. At the beginning, there was anguish and despair about whether he would survive. Then came the fear that he might survive but be left hopelessly disabled. In circumstances like this it is not uncommon for family members to wonder whether their loved one would be better off dead. With those thoughts can come a terrible sense of disbelief and guilt that continues to gnaw especially when survival is associated with an ongoing gratitude for life irrespective of its challenges.

Carlos had been the man, the family leader, a powerful presence, and, of course, the breadwinner. After the accident, he needed to rediscover and redefine himself—as did all the members of his family as they dealt with the continuous fallout from what had happened. For him, the loss was physical and psychological—obviously his eye, but thankfully we have two, and his mobility. Carlos was in a wheelchair for months. Many said he would never walk again but walk he did. First with the help of a frame, the kind my 83-year-old mother used before she died, then perched on two crutches as he dragged his floppy feet. Months later, with the help of two sticks, he was up on those feet walking with a high-stepping gait and then, a long time later, with just one stick for balance. Now, a decade and a half later, he is walking unaided.

Unlike true paraplegics, who lose continuity of their spinal cord and for whom there is no readily available treatment to restore their ability to walk, Carlos' paralysis was caused by crush injuries to both his sciatic nerves. The injuries occurred as a result of the pressure effect of all that blood along with the shearing movement of the pelvic bones crushing the nerve roots that form both the right and left sciatic nerves. Those nerve roots emerge from the spinal cord on both sides, then travel through windows in the bony pelvis to join up, forming the left and right sciatic nerves. Like the Amazon River, the sciatic is the longest and widest single nerve in the human body, running from the top of the leg to the back of the foot. It is responsible for the feeling we sense on most of the back of our thigh, the front of the lower leg, and the entire foot. Without it, the muscles of the back of the thigh and those of the leg and foot simply won't work.

Carlos says I saved his life. I certainly played my part, but he is here today because of the efforts of many, not least himself and his family. In the time he was with us there were many more close calls, occasions when he seemed to be making good progress only to be set back by a complication. In the beginning, these individual battles were fought for every single advance—being able to breathe for himself; sustain his own blood pressure without help from drugs; absorbing the liquid diet we delivered down his nasogastric tube; swallowing food while he was still breathing through a tracheostomy tube. Everything was a challenge; every moment of every day there was always another hill to climb. Two steps forward some days, three steps back on others. Every inch gained came with effort and a fight. Despite our attempts to smooth the ride for Carlos, Sandy rode this rollercoaster from hell with him too—the ups and the downs and the twists and the turns. Wisely, she kept a diary of those times.

Intensive care patients like Carlos are exposed to a series of terrifying near-death experiences, caused by their accident or illness and also by what it takes to get them better. Almost all of them will have recurring nightmares and dreams, and many will have symptoms of a classic post-traumatic stress disorder—unexplained and recurrent panic attacks, depression, fear, anger, sadness, pain, as well as a range of flashbacks in which unreal memories can come back in very real ways.

In more recent times, patient diaries have proved to be a simple, no cost, and powerful means to explain and prevent the progression of many of these symptoms. Most importantly perhaps, they allow confused and scrambled patients to better understand their feelings by connecting them to the reality of what actually happened while they were so ill. Some studies show that patients may even be able to distinguish between reality and imagination, and determine whether some of those memories are misinterpretations of what actually happened. Sandy was way ahead of her time.

During Carlos' stay with us, I asked several times whether I could read her diary. I thought that it would help us better understand what she and her children were going through, thus helping us to help her and others in the future. However, she always said no. I don't ask people this anymore because I know that these diaries remain a deeply personal and private record of a harrowing time and, as such, are none of my business. I think it served her well whatever was in it.

It's hard to believe that anyone can survive the physical trauma that Carlos suffered. That he did speaks volumes about him as a person. Recently, on a fine sunny afternoon, Carlos, Sandy and I met for lunch at a Grey Lynn restaurant. It had been well over a year since our last date so we had lots to catch up on. It was a terrific afternoon of reflection and ongoing reconciliation. At one point, Carlos said that despite his difficulties—and there have been many—he would never wish to turn the clock back.

He said he is now more at ease with himself and a better man than he would ever have become without the accident. Carlos is a glass half-full kind of guy, but that means more than him just being blindly optimistic. He is content by design, not by luck. I came away feeling happy—happy to see them so together and in that moment of their lives—and privileged to have been part of this inspirational journey.

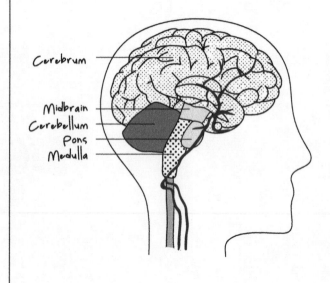

the Brain and the Brain Stem

Cerebrum

Midbrain
Cerebellum
Pons
Medulla

CHAPTER 7

The ultimate gift—

life

EARLY ONE MORNING A few years ago, I drove to the hospital to visit a good friend and his brother, both patients on the renal transplant ward. The streets were empty, so too were the hospital corridors. I was there for a celebration to be marked by the three of us watching the live broadcast of a rugby game, a test match between the All Blacks and South Africa in Johannesburg.

The story had started several months before when Trevor, my friend's brother, turned up in the emergency department of the hospital close to death. He hadn't been well for some time and was becoming increasingly tired and lethargic. Earlier that afternoon, he had visited an oral surgeon to seek advice about a white lesion on his tongue. Thinking it might be an oral cancer, the surgeon took a small biopsy of the lesion and sent Trevor on his way. Within a few minutes Trevor's tongue began to bleed, quite quickly becoming dark in colour and twice its normal size. Already in their car and realising the danger he was in, his wife drove at breakneck speed to my hospital. When they arrived in the emergency department, Trevor was in deep trouble; his tongue was so swollen that the only airway he had was thanks to the tiny space created by his finger pushing his tongue down off the roof of his mouth.

He was immediately transferred to the operating theatres for expert help to secure his airway and save his life. He was met there by an anaesthetist, a surgeon, and nurses. The plan was simple—do an awake fibre-optic intubation. Should that fail, or if Trevor lost his airway beforehand, the surgeon was there and ready to do an emergency tracheostomy.

Trevor was attached to some monitors, a drip was put in, and bloods taken. Sue, the anaesthetist, sprayed his nose with local anaesthetic while an assistant prepared the small-bore flexible bronchoscope. This is a clever device, a narrow tube with a camera on its end, which is advanced through the nose, across the back of the pharynx, round the corner at the back of the tongue and forward toward the larynx. All the way down, she sprayed more local to stop Trevor gagging and coughing and make this uncomfortable procedure as bearable as possible. The bronchoscope is sufficiently small for a breathing tube to be preloaded onto it. Once Sue negotiated the way through the vocal cords into the top of the trachea the breathing tube was advanced off the bronchoscope, giving Trevor a safe airway. This sounds easy but it isn't. With every breath and cough, the tissues move and the view from the scope's camera is lost. Thankfully, on this occasion, all went according to plan and without too much difficulty.

Once Trevor was safe, he was sedated and transferred to the ICU, which is where I saw him the next morning. I remember being stunned when I saw his bloods. The creatinine level in his blood, a marker of renal function, was over 1000—the normal range is 60 to 110. His urea, a waste product normally excreted by the kidneys, was 60—the normal range is four to eight—and he was anaemic. I knew immediately that Trevor had end-stage renal failure. No wonder his tongue bled! With a urea level that high, our platelets, which normally prevent bleeding, don't work. And as for that white lesion on his tongue, that was no cancer—it was what we call uraemic glossitis, another sign of severe renal failure.

I found out later that Trevor's family had a history of poly-cystic kidney disease, a genetic disorder that results from a mutation in our DNA which can be passed from one generation to the next. His grandfather, father and two sisters had died of this. Trevor knew a fair bit about his disease and the nature of its transmission and although he was being monitored by a renal physician, the rapid deterioration in his kidney function and this weird complication had taken everyone by surprise.

The pattern of inheritance here is one we call autosomal dominant, a form of Russian roulette, where a child can get the disorder by inheriting the gene mutation from only one parent. Each child of a parent with an autosomal dominant mutation therefore has a 50 per cent chance of inheriting the abnormal gene. My close friend Rod, Trevor's brother, was spared.

The swelling in Trevor's tongue quickly reduced so after a couple of days we took out his breathing tube and discharged him to the care of the renal service. A week later, Trevor went home but this time with a large-bore dialysis catheter in his neck and instructions to return three times a week.

In the meantime, Rod was making his own plans to donate a kidney to his brother and had contacted the live donor service to begin the exhaustive set of investigations to allow this to happen safely for both of them. The process culminated in the 'operations' a few days before the early morning test match.

There we were waiting for the rugby to start at three in the morning in Rod's hospital room. The TV was set up, the tea made, and soon Trevor arrived from his room next door. His new kidney safely tucked into a superficial space in his left anterior abdominal wall, he was smiling, sartorial with his hospital gown gaping at the back, as he pushed a pole on which hung his IV fluids and a bag full of urine.

However, Rod was not so excited at the prospect of watching the rugby. He was barely awake, drowsy and snoring from the morphine dose necessary to control the pain from his operation. Those were the days before the now much less painful removal of a donor's kidney through a keyhole incision using a laparoscope. Swooping down Rod's side was a long, Praxiteles-like wound closing the deep tunnel made by the surgeons to gain access into his retroperitoneum in order to remove one of his kidneys. How ironic, I thought—Trevor looking so chipper, his catheter bag bulging with urine from his brother's kidney and poor Rod out to it and oblivious to the drama unfolding at Ellis Park.

In most parts of the world there are more people waiting for organs than there are organs available for transplantation. Many will wait for months, some for years, and some will die waiting. In New Zealand, there are about 600 people waiting for transplants, two-thirds of them on dialysis waiting for a kidney, and the rest super urgently needing a heart, a lung or a liver immediately necessary to save their lives.

For people with end-stage renal failure, longevity and quality of life on dialysis are to a large extent related to the underlying disease process at work. Unlike Trevor, the majority of people on dialysis have end-stage renal failure as a result of diabetes. As such, they are not well because of the widespread vascular disease that accompanies it. For them, life on dialysis is both tough and short.

For Trevor, if done well, dialysis could have been very effective, but we knew that a live kidney transplant would be much better, allowing him to live an independent and active life.

Donating a kidney to someone you know as Rod did is called directed donation. It ensures that the kidney goes to a specific individual. Donating to a stranger is called altruistic or non-directed donation and, in this case, the kidney will be given to the next best-matched patient on the waiting list.

Notwithstanding the story of my friend, a good number of donated organs are the result of more tragic circumstances, from people who suffer a severe injury to their brain and become brain dead. They also come from a smaller group of patients with a severe brain injury who do not become brain dead but die within an hour of being removed from a ventilator.

Diane had suffered from brittle asthma all her life—a form of the disease that is severe, unpredictable and often recurrent. As a child, she'd had many admissions to hospital but by the time she became a teenager, she was better settled on steroid inhalers and Ventolin and her breathing seemed to improve. However, one day, quite suddenly when she was alone at home she had a severe asthma attack. Despite using her home nebuliser she did not improve. Breathless and gasping, she called an ambulance. By the time the paramedics arrived, she was unconscious and in cardiac arrest, the flatline of asystole showing on the monitor. The paramedics began CPR, took over her breathing, and gave her several rounds of intravenous adrenaline. After twenty minutes, her heart started but she remained totally comatose. Diane was eighteen years old.

Strangely, when she arrived at hospital twenty minutes later and we listened to her chest, there was no sign of the tight wheeze that had caused her collapse and on first glance she looked so peaceful that a bystander could have thought that she was simply asleep. Tragically that was not the case. Despite all that we did to improve her condition, the damage was done and after 48 hours, it was evident that Diane had become brain dead.

Tavita was a property developer and farmer from down south. He was a fit and healthy man who loved nothing more than working on the land. Early one morning, he and his two sons were shaping a new road on the edge of their property. Tavita was at the helm of a large earthmoving machine when its accelerator jammed and the huge machine left the road. He jumped off and landed awkwardly, the back of his head hitting the ground with an audible thump. By the time his boys got to him he was deeply unconscious but still breathing. Paramedics arrived soon after, stabilised his neck in a stiff collar, intubated him, and raced to hospital.

On arrival, Tavita had a Glasgow Coma score of three—as low as it gets—and fixed and dilated pupils. Apart from the blow to the head, he had no other injuries. A CT done soon after painted a grim picture. The normal structures of his brain were no longer evident; it looked more like a watermelon after it had been dropped, so bad was the swelling and bleeding. A day or so later, he too was declared brain dead.

Moana was 52. She worked in the city for a high-powered law firm. At a meeting one morning she complained of a sudden and severe headache. She said it felt like she had been hit across the head with a baseball bat. Inside her head, a small aneurysm on a big artery had suddenly burst. Moments later she collapsed to the ground and never woke again. Like Diane and Tavita, Moana also became brain dead.

These are tragic and sad stories and of course there have been and will be many others. Each is the result of something unexpected and sudden that brings with it a kind of grief and shock that is impossible to describe.

Diane, Tavita and Moana all suffered catastrophic neurological consequences associated with a sudden and progressive increase in pressure inside the cranium to the point when that intracranial pressure exceeds the arterial pressure taking blood into the brain. At that point, the brain loses its blood supply causing the brain and brainstem, the very top segment of the spinal cord, to die. This is accompanied by well-recognised physiological changes and neurological findings that are evident on bedside examination and it is these that are used to diagnose brain death—a state where there is an irreversible loss of brain and brainstem function. Following agonising discussions with their families, all three agreed to organ donation.

Each year in New Zealand, another forty or so people join them, the majority dying from a sudden cerebral haemorrhage like Moana, others from trauma like Tavita, and a smaller number as a result of a severe hypoxic injury to the brain like Diane's.

For everyone's protection, making the diagnosis of brain death is clearly and strictly defined in guidelines determined by world bodies of intensive care and other professional bodies. In all cases, there is an accepted set of conditions and diagnostic tests to confirm this condition before organ donation can proceed. In this part of the world it is the Australian and New Zealand Intensive Care Society (ANZICS) that sets these guidelines in accordance with evidence and best practice from around the world. Getting to this point has been an interesting journey with many ethical, moral and legal twists and turns along the way.

How we define death has continued to change over the years. Before we accumulated a detailed knowledge of anatomy and physiology, death was signalled when the soul departed the body. With greater knowledge about the function of the heart and circulation, death was said to have occurred when the heart stopped beating and there was no forward flow of blood. Now we recognise death as a process in which different cells of the body may cease to function at different rates. Its definition is complicated further because we know that artificial respiration for patients who cannot adequately breathe for themselves can keep the heart beating, thereby sustaining life in other organs of the body once the brain is dead.

For people like Diane, Tavita and Moana, who have suffered a catastrophic neurological event, artificial ventilation and other kinds of organ support are not only used to buy time to diagnose, provide care, determine prognosis and allow family and loved ones to gather and come to terms with what is going, but also to give them time to discuss organ donation with their families.

The actual diagnosis of brain death must be made by two medical practitioners and is, in effect, a diagnosis of death. The time that brain death is determined becomes the official time of death recorded on a death certificate, despite a patient's body still being kept alive in an intensive care unit.

Diane, Tavita and Moana had all collapsed suddenly and within seconds lost any chance of recovery. For their families, this was a time of overwhelming shock and disbelief. Their grief is palpable and their emotions raw. It is a time that brings families and friends together to support each other, putting aside many of the things that may have kept them apart before. It is a deep dive into uncharted emotional territory in which great distances are covered in a short space of time. At some stage in this torment, when the winds begin to settle and with the right facilitation, it can become a time for reconciliation of differences, reminiscing and, later, a time for some humour too.

We, the doctors and nurses, travel that distance alongside families doing what we can to help, inform and comfort them. It is a time for truth-telling because there is no turning the clock back. None of us are Superman able to spin the earth backwards in order to turn back time and save Lois Lane's life. We live in the real world.

Right from the start, the conversations we have set the tone for what's to follow. Never easy, these need as much care and preparation as if part of a surgical procedure. How we proceed together is determined by how well we connect, and the way that we recognise and address the things that really matter. We have come a very long way since that day when my father, out of huge frustration at the limited but strictly enforced visiting hours, climbed the drainpipe at Wellington Hospital to get a glimpse of my brother Les lying there in traction. That hospital treated my father badly and he never forgave them for that.

What you reap is what you sow. Kindness, compassion, expertise and honesty deliver great rewards when it comes to hard conversations. So too does time spent to help families better understand what has happened and what the consequences of those things are, especially when a terrible outcome is expected. In practical terms, that may mean we meet formally with families many times in one day and, in between, have more conversations with small groups or individuals to get people to a common understanding. Coming to terms with a terrible truth takes time and it is our job to help that process along.

As we get a better sense of the patient's condition and prognosis, what we discuss in the more formal family meetings evolves over time. I do my best to be totally transparent when it comes to sharing information to help families come to terms with what has occurred and to better understand what I am saying. If I suspect there is a chance that a patient might become brain dead, I will usually mention that as a possibility. Commonly families will pick up on this and, if it is appropriate, then we will embark on a more detailed conversation. With Diane's family this process was prolonged and delicate.

There can be no such thing as 'normal' or 'expected' behaviour from parents about to lose a child. Other issues can make the process all the more complicated. In Diane's case, her mother and father had separated several years earlier and it was clear from the outset that they didn't get on. She spent time with each of them in a shared care arrangement. One week with her dad, who had remarried and now lived with his new wife and her three children, and the next week with her mum in the old family home. When she collapsed, Diane was at her mother's house. Sadly she was alone as her mother was at work.

After 36 hours with us in the ICU, despite the breathing tube, drips and monitors, Diane still looked like Diane. Her hair recently washed, she looked even more peaceful than she had when she was first admitted. By this time I had met and spoken with her family many times and they now seemed much closer to accepting the possibility that Diane may not do well.

Even though it was not common practice then, I asked the family whether they would consider joining me and a colleague as we did a further formal assessment of Diane's neurological state and level of consciousness. They agreed but before going ahead we found ourselves in another conversation about brain death and organ donation.

At that time, I strongly suspected Diane had become brain dead but it was her mother who raised the possibility of her becoming an organ donor. There is no one right time to broach such a sensitive issue with a family in a position like this, but the right time always becomes obvious, at least it does to me. When that time comes I do what I can to provide families with as much information as I can so they can make the right decision for them. Despite always being an advocate for donation, in the early part of my career success was defined by a family agreeing to organ donation and failure by their refusal, but with time I have become less invested in the outcome, wanting only to do the right thing by the family carrying the awful burden of this sudden loss.

With my registrar and Diane's estranged parents in the room, we prepared to do the formal tests to confirm brain death. Although I have done this many times before, I took even greater care to demonstrate that we were meticulously following the protocols and guidelines, explaining each as we went.

This standardised approach provides the public—and all involved—with reassurance about the process and protects its integrity. Before we can even start making an assessment whether brain death might have occurred, there are a series of questions that need to be answered. The answers to these questions ensure that the diagnosis is sound; that the patient has indeed suffered an irreversible loss of brainstem function and has become brain dead. Once that has been proven, should the family agree to organ donation, the process of identifying potential recipients and harvesting the deceased person's organs prior to them being transplanted begins.

This is goose bump territory because once done, it unleashes a man-made chain of events that is fuelled by integrity, evidence and good will from all parties. In reality, it is a series of processes that move in many directions, touching and calling on the expertise of many people, often in different parts of a country or across countries. It is profound, moving and magnificent and it starts with an informed, heartfelt 'Yes, we agree'.

The brainstem is an ancient and essential part of our neurological system. Anatomically, it is the connection between the brain and our spinal cord, the home of functions vital to life and the highway along which all signals travel from our body to our brain and from our brain to our body. It is also the home of many of the cranial nerves, which control how our eyes work, our swallow and cough reflex, whether we can initiate a breath or not and much more.

As complex as all that is, assessing cranial nerve function at the bedside is a relatively simple thing to do and it is this assessment that is used to diagnose brain death.

The diagnosis can only be made by demonstrating the complete and irreversible loss of function of every single one of those cranial nerves while excluding a range of other conditions that might confound our findings.

With Diane's parents present and watching, we carefully ticked off the preconditions and, one by one, ruled out those other causes:

1. We had been closely observing and monitoring Diane in an intensive care unit for longer than six hours, a sign of irreversibility.
2. We were certain of the diagnosis that she had suffered a severe brain injury from a lack of oxygen (or hypoxia) as a result of her asthma attack and the prolonged period of cardiac arrest associated with it. Repeated

examinations by many of us, and the CT findings, showed features that clearly matched the diagnosis.

3. Diane's temperature was in the normal range for testing—a very low body temperature can itself confuse our testing.

4. There was no evidence of other conditions that could confound the findings from the tests we were about to perform, especially those that resulted from the effects of sedative or other medications.

5. The rest of Diane's blood tests were normal, ruling out other important conditions caused by electrolyte, endocrine and metabolic disturbances that could make bedside testing less accurate in diagnosing brain death.

6. We agreed that at no stage had Diane been given neuromuscular-blocking drugs to prevent her moving spontaneously or reacting to any other sort of stimulus which would confound the testing.

7. And finally, because she was still quite stable from a respiratory point of view, it was straightforward to examine her cranial nerves and do the apnoea test to ensure that she had irreversibly lost the ability to breathe.

While all of this was going on, Diane remained unchanged, deeply comatose on a ventilator, all her vital signs stable, while her nurse, always at the bedside, attended to the myriad of tasks necessary to keep her free of complications.

For Diane to be declared brain dead, she needed to show no response to any of the tests we were about to embark on and those tests needed to be done twice in the presence of two doctors. So with her parents watching and me giving a running commentary, we went through each of the eight bedside tests for the first time.

First, we tested to see whether Diane showed any sign of consciousness by seeing whether she responded, in any way at all, to a painful stimulus in the area of the cranial nerves. This was done by applying pressure to the area where the supraoptic nerve exits the skull—at a point that is roughly in the middle of each eyebrow. I then applied pressure to the nail beds of a finger and toe on each limb. In each instance, Diane did not flinch or show any physiological response whatsoever to these painful stimuli.

Next, we examined her pupils. Since admission, these had been fixed and dilated—fixed in that they did not constrict to a bright light and dilated because they were the size of saucers. We tested each eye for any direct response to light—there was none. We then shone a light in one eye looking for constriction of the pupil in the other eye, the so-called consensual light reflex. That too was absent.

Next, we tested the corneal or blink reflex. The blink is one of our most rapid and powerful reflexes. It is so quick that in a flash-burn to the face—common in summer when young men throw a light onto a petrol-soaked woodpile—the eyes are rarely injured, while the rest of the face is singed. I opened Diane's eyes one at a time and with the edge of a gauze swab, touched the cornea, the surface of the eye over the pupil. There was no blink. What I saw and felt was much more than a simple absence of a reflex; Diane was gone, her eyes were devoid of life like those of a fish on ice. Within them I saw only the profound emptiness of death.

Following that, we tested for the loss of integrity of the vestibulo-ocular reflex, a complex set of connections between a number of cranial nerves that control eye movement and balance. Done on one side then the other, 50 to 100 millilitres of ice cold water is slowly injected into the ear canal. An assistant then holds open both eyelids while we watch for any movements of the eyes. In a conscious person, the normal response would be to see both eyes move together toward the side of the stimulation, then flick back to the centre. Diane's eyes, still as big as saucers, stared blankly upward. They did not move. They did nothing.

Next, we tested for a gag reflex. Using a small wooden tongue depressor, I carefully touched both sides of the back of her throat at the level of the pharynx. Normally this would evoke a powerful gag, a reflex designed to protect us from inhaling food and other material into our lungs. Once again, these were absent.

Our cough reflex is another survival mechanism, which is easy to assess. I opened up a port at the end of Diane's breathing tube and slipped a long suction catheter, normally used to retrieve secretions, deep into her trachea. Diane made no effort to cough.

Brain death is always associated with a total loss of respiratory function even in the face of the most powerful physiological stimulus to breathe—a defined and much higher than normal level of carbon dioxide in our blood. To avoid hypoxia, we raised the oxygen level in Diane's blood before removing her from the ventilator then, through a similar suction catheter that was used in the previous test, we ran a flow of one to two litres of oxygen a minute into her breathing tube to keep her oxygen saturations above 90 per cent, all the while paying close attention to see whether she made any respiratory effort as the carbon dioxide level in her blood slowly rose. As time passed the level of carbon dioxide in her blood started to rise. At several points, we measured the partial pressure of carbon dioxide in Diane's blood to ensure that we reached the level of 60 millimetres of Mercury (mmHg) or 8.5 kilo Pascals (kPa) defined in the guideline. After eight minutes, her carbon dioxide level came back at 75 milli-metres of mHg or 10 kPa, well above that threshold. At no stage during that process did Diane make any respiratory effort whatsoever.

I carefully documented the results of those tests and spoke with Diane's parents. A little while later, again in their presence, we repeated the same set of tests and got the same results. Diane showed no response at all to those tests, which concluded at twenty past midnight—the official time of Diane's death. That time together with the diagnosis of brain death would later feature on the official record, given to her family the next morning.

Not long after, we had our last formal family meeting, me, Diane's parents, her stepfather, a grandparent, her sister, a brother, and an uncle and aunt. Diane was dead. My job now was to get the best result for this family—something that in one month, three months, a year, and forever, at the worst, they could live with without regret.

It didn't take long before they spoke about what Diane would have wanted for herself. She had been a wonderful daughter and, despite the divorce and the difficulties that followed, she loved her parents, as they had loved her. They described her as generous to a fault, always putting others before herself. Although they had never talked about the possibility of some-thing like this occurring and had never spoken about organ donation, it was something her family knew she would want to do. I said nothing and listened. One by one they spoke, looking at each other with tears in their eyes, seemingly united again as a family.

I thanked them. They had made an extremely brave decision. Although Diane was dead and able to be removed from the venti-lator, after which her heart would slow and within minutes stop, they elected to prolong this inevitable process. They agreed to keep Diane on the ventilator to allow for a myriad of new tests to be done in order to assess the function of her heart, lungs, liver, kidneys and potentially other transplantable tissues too. This would take many more hours. Despite her youth, the longer that took, the more likely Diane's body, adrift without its brain, might begin to unwind in strange ways.

We discussed this possibility in some detail, that Diane might need to be actively warmed to prevent her becoming significantly hypothermic, and that she would likely require further boluses of intravenous fluids and drug infusions to support her blood pressure as well as other drugs to correct endocrine abnormalities commonly associated with brain death.

I took particular care to explain a weird and deeply disturbing complication associated with brain death—abnormal movements of the limbs and sometimes the head that can sometimes occur in this setting. These are spinal reflex movements, just like the involuntary knee jerk that occurs after a knock to the patella tendon just below a bent knee.

These so-called spinal reflexes can also be initiated in other muscle groups in our arms and elsewhere but are not spontaneously evident in the presence of a normally functioning nervous system. With the onset of brain death and loss of the normal hierarchy of neurological control mechanisms, these spinal reflex movements can occur spontaneously and become pronounced. They are not signs of life.

Despite explaining the possibility of this in advance, when they occur these movements can be deeply unsettling for families and raise in them renewed hope of a miraculous recovery.

Despite the family's agreeing to Diane becoming a donor, we also talked about the rare occurrence when something from left field might arise to prevent donation from occurring—a technical issue, an undiagnosed disease in the donor or an unusual problem with the recipients. As rare as this is, it gives me the opportunity to thank them for their willingness to donate, for the journey they have taken to acknowledge what Diane would have wanted, and for the courage to follow through whether donation itself takes place or not. I tell them this is all they can do, they have embraced it wholeheartedly, and I hope that in the future it will bring them strength.

In the meantime, I had phoned the donor coordinator who manages the process of donation, setting in motion the well-oiled wheels of a great system. Diane's blood was sent for tissue typing. An echo of her heart was done. Measurements and further tests were taken to assess the size and function of the liver, lungs and kidneys. All the while a series of phone calls with other specialists and the donor coordinator took place to help finesse the process.

At the same time, a separate part of the transplant team contacted potential recipients. Some were local, some in far-off places. For them and their families, it is a time of great hope and trepidation. For those waiting for a kidney, life is tough but it is often stable. With this offer comes new problems—a lifetime of drugs to prevent the recipient's body rejecting the foreign tissue of someone else's body and other consequences too. But, like it did for my friend's brother, receiving a new kidney carries the hope of a much more normal life. It is a gift like no other and those lucky enough to receive it profoundly know that. For those waiting for a liver or a heart, organ donation is simply lifesaving and often delay means death.

During this process, most of Diane's family said their goodbyes but her mum and dad decided to stay to see it through. The donor coordinator, the glue that holds all of this together, arrived first to thank them and then to answer any questions that they might have. An hour or so later, at about 5 a.m., the retrieval team arrived—several surgeons and an anaesthetist. Together we went through the paperwork to ensure all was as it should be and, a little while later, Diane was taken to the operating room. Her parents were exhausted, almost too tired to cry. I was exhausted too. By that stage, it seemed like we had known each other for years, but it had only been a day and a half. We spoke together for the last time, hugged each other—yes, there were a few tears—and then we said our goodbyes.

The next morning, we found out that one kidney went to a patient in a town in the far south of the country. He was just 24 years old and doing so well that the kidney was already making urine! The second kidney stayed closer by and went a man in his fifties—it was the same good news for him too.

Diane's heart and one lung were transplanted into a nineteen-year-old girl with cystic fibrosis. Although still on a ventilator, she too was doing well.

One lobe of Diane's liver was transplanted into a three-month-old baby born with an abnormality of the bile ducts. The other went into a 42-year-old mother of three who had quite suddenly developed fulminant liver failure from a viral infection. Both would have been dead in days had their conditions been left untreated, but now they were doing well too. Diane's family would have heard the same news.

I understand only too well how emotionally draining and all-consuming this whole process can be. It is real beyond description. Each time I go through it, I am totally consumed by it and each time it leaves me completely wrung out. I know this is the same for other ICU specialists too.

As for the families, although I cannot speak for them, I have observed in some an overwhelming desire to know more about the recipients—who can assume a new role, as surrogate family in the minds of the donor family. This carries great risks for all parties, so we actively discourage breaking the confidentiality around this process while still maintaining a duty of care to those families. This will vary from one jurisdiction to another but may take the form of occasional or regular calls to ensure that they are doing ok and, if not, they are offered help.

Every year memorial services are held in the bigger cities to honour and remember those who have passed and those who have given and received. For everyone involved, living has a new meaning.

Each year in New Zealand, on average, forty people will become brain dead and donate organs. A much smaller number of patients with a severe unrecoverable brain injury, who do not develop brain death but die within an hour of them being removed from a ventilator, will do the same. Although each one is a momentous event, in the bigger scheme of things, the demand for organs far outweighs the supply. This is especially so for the fabulous kidney, slowly failing in more and more people as a result of the epidemic of obesity-related diabetes.

From time to time, usually in response to publicity about a single case, politicians come under pressure to increase donor numbers and look to other jurisdictions for ideas. Spain leads the way internationally with 34 deceased donors per million popula-tion—3.4 times the rate of donors in New Zealand—according to figures from the International Registry of Organ Donation and Transplantation.

Although different factors impact on these differing donor rates, it is the legal environment, and organisational and cultural issues, that seem to be most important. Spain, Belgium and Portugal have all passed 'presumed consent' laws where individuals are automatically considered an organ donor unless they opt out. Other jurisdictions have established donor registers to allow individuals to opt in. Both have their downsides: inaction in an opt-in system can lead to individuals who would want to be a donor not donating. In contrast, inaction in an opt-out system can potentially lead to an individual who does not want to donate becoming a donor, or a family deeply opposed to donation feeling as though the state has stolen the organs of their loved one. In each case, the ramifications for families, also grappling with the tragedy of death, can be disastrous.

Spain's presumed consent laws have helped improve rates of organ donation, but their success in large part has been attributed to the organisational measures it has implemented. In 1989, Spain established a nationwide transplant coordination network. It helps doctors and transplant coordinators to identify potential donors through better training and education. It also provides real-time advice to treating clinicians.

A similar system has been established in New Zealand through Organ Donation New Zealand, but for strong cultural reasons we require family consent for organ donation to proceed in order to protect the ongoing interests of the surviving family.

Organ donation in circumstances like Diane's results from a sudden and unexpected catastrophe and therefore something many people have not considered. Despite that, we can and should make our own wishes known about what we might want for ourselves by speaking with family and friends. These are conversations we really ought to have along with those about what matters to us about how we live and how we wish to die. These don't have to be morbid and sad; on the contrary they are more about life than death. Most of all, they should help us all get the most out of this gift—our one and only precious life.

The Liver, Gallbladder and
Bile Duct

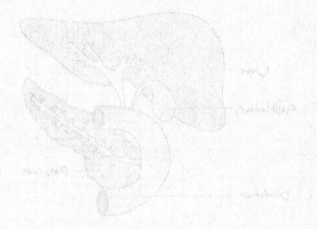

Liver

Gallbladder

Pancreas

Duodenum

the Liver, Gallbladder and Bile Duct

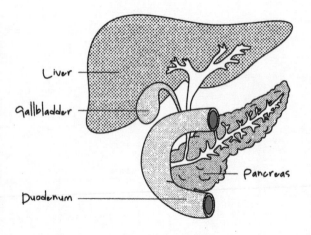

The art of medicine—

less is more

CHAPTER 8

The art of medicine

less is more

MARY WAS 78. SHE lived with her only daughter not far from the rugby stadium in town, very close to the port. Together they managed a small hotel frequented by visiting teams and their families as well as ordinary tourists to this small Pacific island. There were eight rooms upstairs all with verandahs and terrific views looking out to the northwest over the bay. The ones at the front looked directly onto the port where the newly arrived yachts came in to moor or seek shelter, then across to the wharf that was often obscured by mammoth cruise liners that came and went either side of the cyclone season.

Mary had been a fit woman. She worked hard and apart from smoking briefly when she was in her twenties, she had led a healthy life. Her daily routine seemed to have been a mix of work and pleasure—cleaning in the morning, socialising with her friends in the afternoon, and doing bookwork in the evening. She had only one child, unusual in these parts, due to the premature death of her husband in an accident at sea when her daughter was three.

Ten years before I met her, Mary had travelled to New Zealand to have her gallbladder removed following several bouts of cholecystitis. In the subsequent years she had slowed up quite a bit, becoming overweight and, with that, increasingly sedentary and more tired. Work that she had managed to do without much effort in the past became more burdensome and, in the end, she spent more and more time at the front desk and less time on her feet moving about. Mary had lived a good life but her world had shrunk to the point that she was now quite limited in what she could do.

We met in the medical ward of the small hospital. I had been asked to see her by a young doctor worried about how she was doing. Mary had been admitted the previous evening with a fever and a five-day history of right-sided upper abdominal pain, profuse diarrhoea, dehydration and acute renal failure.

When I saw her that morning, her daughter Kara was with her. Together, we reviewed the events of the past few days, including their visit to a local GP to seek help and an explanation for the pain. He had thought Mary was constipated and prescribed her laxatives. Thinking they would help, Mary had taken them by the handful, ending up with days of diarrhoea and profound dehydration prior to her hospital admission.

When I examined her in more detail, she was confused, feverish and sore. The pain and tenderness was mostly on her right side, at the top of her abdomen where the liver lives. Although she was breathing well, Mary was still under-resuscitated. Her tongue was dry, she was thirsty, and she wasn't making much urine. Her heart was racing, her blood pressure was low, and her hands and feet were cold.

The blood tests that had been done the previous evening suggested she might have an infection affecting her liver and bile ducts because she had a raised white blood cell count and a non-specific derangement of her liver enzymes with a mildly elevated bilirubin. As a result of all of those things Mary's creatinine was elevated, signalling that her kidneys were failing.

Despite the efforts of the medical team overnight, Mary was still incredibly sick, most likely from infection compounded by the effects of dehydration and shock. Without more aggressive treatment she would surely die but just how aggressive that treatment should be was the question we needed to discuss because, at her age and stage, I didn't think she would survive a round of full-bore intensive care.

Of course, there was a time when no such discussion would take place, no explanation would be given, and decisions would be made by a medical team who knew what was best—'don't you worry your pretty little head about it, dear'. These decisions weren't necessarily wrong, but they seldom took into account the thoughts, concerns and desires of the patients and their families. Nor did the people making them see the benefits of taking families with them as these important questions were decided.

Thankfully, the tide has turned on that kind of thinking and in the twenty-first century, clinicians are expected to share their thoughts with patients and their families and doctors are expected to spend time with them, to judge together what the best course of action might be for any one patient. This approach is liberating for all parties because, unlike the certainty of death and taxes, medicine has few blacks and whites, just endless shades of grey, multiple possibilities and some probabilities following any course of action.

Diagnosis and treatment are as much an art as they are a science, and the final result may not in fact be final because of ongoing changes in how patients respond to their treatment over time. This is the context in which we operate—this is the art of medicine where we know what we know and we apply what we know, see what we get and make adjustments as necessary to get the best for each and every patient. There is an honesty in this approach that does not need to be confusing or unintelligible; it just needs to be recognised and talked about.

This more open and collaborative approach between patients and their doctors is a world away from the arrogance of certainty that was such a big part of medical practice when I first started. Now that I am in the mid-afternoon of my career, it seems that medicine might become what I always wanted it to be: a true partnership between those intimately involved.

These thoughts and many more were swirling in my head when I finished my examination and prepared to speak with Kara. For my part, the easiest thing of all would have been for me to go all out for Mary's survival by pulling the trigger on every technology and intervention to treat the underlying condition and fix those bad numbers reported back from the lab. Those interventions would likely include the full-court press you have become familiar with: putting Mary off to sleep, taking over her breathing, inserting a big central line into the jugular vein in her neck or a femoral vein in her groin to give powerful drugs that support her blood pressure, putting her onto a dialysis machine just in case her kidneys didn't recover, and marinating her in antibiotics. Once most of that was done, she would need a series of investigations to determine the exact cause of her problem. A CT scan of her belly at the very least, using intravenous contrast material to outline the various structures to help interpret the pictures, then a plan to intervene as necessary by way of a drainage procedure or even an operation if that was thought to be necessary. In Mary's case, all of that would have been the medical equivalent of the invasion of Iraq—and we all know how well that went. Yes, that was the easy option too: total control but with Rumsfeld-like consequences.

A full-blown course of intensive care is gruelling beyond description. Young people who do well in the short term can take months to recover their physical and emotional strength after a critical illness that requires ventilation and organ support. If we did that to Mary, at worst we would surely kill her or at best she would never get back to anywhere near where she was before she fell ill.

When dealing with frail patients, the elderly, and those with advanced chronic disease, often less is more. In my view, even doing the CT scan carried an unacceptable risk because the intravenous contrast necessary to delineate the images clearly would worsen her renal function and likely push Mary's kidneys beyond the point of recovery. Even if we found the source of her infection—a stricture in her bile duct as a result of her previous gallbladder surgery or an infected collection of fluid in her abdomen—I wasn't sure Mary would survive the interventions necessary to fix them. My sense was to do simple things well and see if she improved. That formed the basis of my discussion with Kara and Mary.

We sat and spoke together for an hour. I explained what I thought was going on and the risks of the different options but it was Kara who did most of the talking while I listened. She told me much more about her mother's life, the ups and downs of hotel life, her love for Kara's three children, her time studying at university in New Zealand. Finally, she spoke in more detail about how Mary spent her days and what she now valued about her life. In a roundabout way, this was how Kara dealt with the information that I was giving her to help decide what she thought Mary would want. In the end we agreed: no heroics, no escalation of care to ventilation if her breathing deteriorated, no dialysis if her kidneys stopped functioning completely, and no CPR if she had a cardiac arrest.

Instead we would tread carefully along the thin line between treatment and torture, keeping Mary's comfort as our number one goal, while doing the simple things well in the hope that she would get better.

Soon after, we moved Mary up to the small ICU on the first floor so we could monitor her progress more closely and do the things we planned. We attached her to some basic monitoring and continued to resuscitate her with fluids. We started a couple of intravenous medications to improve her cardiac function and blood pressure, all of which were given through an existing IV line in her forearm—no big neck lines for her. We broadened her antibiotic cover, then we waited and we watched.

There are millions of patients like Mary living happy, high-quality lives within ever-decreasing circles as their worlds shrink around them as they age and become more infirm. Managing their illnesses to maintain that quality of life is one of the greatest challenges facing modern medicine. It is also one of the most rewarding. Although some of the means to do that better will come from new knowledge and emerging technologies, medicine's greatest achievement will be successfully customising these treatments to the changing needs of those individual patients. This is the pointy end of the art of medicine, a nirvana of medical practice where the right approach for one patient might transform their ability to live their lives as they want to. This is a serious challenge to current medical practice because it requires much more than technical skills and knowledge. What's needed is a genuine interest in the lives of each of our patients, and the patience and wisdom to shape that knowledge to get the results that matter most to them. Currently this is the purview of geriatric medicine and palliative care but this approach clearly needs to extend down across the practice of medicine more generally.

Over the next few hours, Mary improved a little. As I went back and forth across the room from one patient to the next, I'd stop and do a quick end-of-the-bed-o-gram, taking in the things that I needed to see. Her pulse rate was steadily coming down, her blood pressure happily moving in the other direction, and she had a better colour. Her urine bag had started to fill, and when I touched her feet, they seemed to be warmer. All of these were signs of an improved circulation in response to the fluids, drugs and antibiotics. Kara could see that too and we joked that even Mary's spiky grey hair seemed to have a bit more body.

She continued to make slow but steady progress. By the second evening, she was talking sense and starting to drink a little. Her white-cell count, a marker of infection, had dropped back towards normal. Her renal function continued to drift off but at a slower rate than before. Some things just take time to get better and, sure enough, the following morning her blood creatinine level, a marker of renal function, had plateaued and then began to fall. She was heading in the right direction and my job became clearer—to slowly back off and let her sort herself out.

I can't tell you how pleased I was. Kara and Mary had shared so much about their lives, and it looked like they would get most of that back. I was thrilled that we got it right—we made the right call when it could so easily have been a very different story.

Although Mary was very limited in what she could physically do, she was at that stage in her life when she spent more time looking back than looking forward. She was enjoying making sense of all that had happened and what she had done. In almost every way, she was no different from you or me: to our family and friends, we are simply irreplaceable. To be able to help her stay a little longer and continue to do that without her suffering, with less rather than more, gave me an immense sense of satisfaction.

It's not unusual for people I have completely forgotten to approach me and thank me for saving someone's life, often many years ago. Exactly that happened in an airport queue recently. Although flattered, I am always a little embarrassed when this happens. Interestingly, I often get the same thanks for looking after people who die. In each case, I like to feel that the system has done its best for each of those patients and their families and, although some are left grieving, we have dealt with each of them with compassion and clarity.

For those patients who survive and do well, we play a pivotal role in making interventions that might lead to an improvement, and in time that improvement might lead to a recovery. While we might have a box of fancy tricks and a room full of technology, the things that we do just make other things possible. Ultimately whether patients survive and recover is determined far more by them and their pre-existing state of health and well-being.

Acute care doctors like me mostly work in hospitals. We are a mixed bag of people from different specialty groups— surgeons, anaesthetists, physicians, emergency doctors, obstetricians, paediatricians, and intensivists like me. All of us work in teams to provide a 24/7 service to the public. We work on call rosters—days, nights, Christmas holidays, Yom Kippur and Rosh Hashanah, and sometimes even on our own birthday. Experiences like meeting Mary and Kara, and being able to make such a difference to their lives, are amazing but I would be lying to you if I pretended that my job was always full of such joy.

For six years in the 1980s I worked and trained at a London teaching hospital. Back then, it was the Jews and Muslims who always worked Christmas—on top of the 134 hours we did every second week. The week in between was a doddle by comparison; then we only worked 72 hours.

At the same time, I was studying for my first set of postgraduate medical exams and trying to hold down a relationship with a similarly hard-working lawyer who also worked long hours for a law firm that sued doctors!

One Monday night, after a typically miserable weekend on call, I arrived home to a dinner of roast chicken—well, almost, because it wasn't quite cooked. It sat there alone on a big plate, in the centre of the table in the dining room of the fine old Edwardian house we had bought a few years before. There we were, the two of us, and the bird, sitting there in a silence that was deafening. Words were not necessary. Worn out, half-cooked, looking as despondent as me, the bird on that plate said it all.

Despite overwhelming tiredness, I was not so out of tune with the real world not to be able to read the signs. I had gone AWOL, becoming lost at work, drowning at sea. On the odd occasion when I was home, I really wasn't. My mind was always ticking over, wondering how the alveolar gas equation went or trying to remember how to draw the intricate workings of the Manley ventilator. The half-cooked bird and the silence helped me see all that, but a bit too late for my first go at a postgraduate exam.

It was a cool winter's morning when I stepped out onto the front steps of our house on London Fields on my way to Bloomsbury for the oral exam. As I opened the door, a funeral procession slowly passed. One of those dour and grim processions with pale men in frock coats and big hats, one black car after another; as I watched, my heart sank and my head followed. I should have turned around and gone back to bed, because when it was my turn to answer the examiners' questions about things I knew well, I was close to mute. I sat there in an almost trance-like state, my mouth so dry I could hardly talk. All I could think about was getting out of there. I had never failed an exam before and never have since, despite sitting many more over the years. That and the uncooked bird were a wake-up call to me. I was a good doctor but I was going over the edge. I had lost my way, and with it all sense of myself and what really mattered. That had to change and I remembered something my father used to misquote: 'If I am not for myself, who will be for me?'

I was not alone it seemed because many of my junior colleagues at the hospital were in a similar situation. Some coped better, a few worse—one of them, Terry, a lovely guy, ended up killing himself with a drug overdose. Our consultants had survived all of that and, having completed their training, had secured jobs for life. All of them seemed to be reaping the rewards of their hard work, many double-dipping in public and private practice. They drove flash cars and spent their evenings at the opera. Despite all that, they remained kind and were especially good to me when I so obviously needed their help. We are all a product of our upbringing, and we are shaped by our experiences and memories. So when I was overcome and my life was a mess, I stepped back to remember where I was from and who I was, and I vowed that I would never again get into that state.

Both my brother and I visited the mohel on our eighth day, and we grew up in a Jewish household. Among friends, I still jokingly describe myself as a Polish Jewish aristocrat. My father had lived under the constant gaze of his grandfather, the Chief Rabbi of Poland, and during his early years he lived an observant life. My mother, an only child, also had an orthodox beginning.

In New Zealand, ours was a Jewish house. Yes, on the right-hand doorpost at the entrance was the mezuzah, a piece of parchment inscribed with the verses of the prayer Shema Yisrael, which was contained in a small, plain, metal case. We celebrated the Jewish holidays with the same gusto as we did those of the goyim. We ate chopped liver and drank borscht. My mother made gefilte fish and in our fridge was a constant supply of herrings, pickled gherkins and smoked eel. I dined on sauerkraut with caraway seeds, Polish potatoes, Wiener schnitzel with horse-radish, and I took sandwiches with strange fillings to school. At night, when I was overly boisterous, my mother gave me ice cream—with brandy. The house was full of mad Europeans who played poker and drank too much. My mother and Aunt Nina smoked constantly and always, there was cake.

We were Jewish to the core but were we religious? Hell no! 'Where was G-d when we needed him?' my parents would ask. 'G-d is a creation of man, not the other way around,' my father would repeat. My father repeated lots of things—especially jokes he was particularly fond of. One of his favourites was reliably retold every year, 194 km north of Wellington, as we drove to our summer holiday destination. Anticipating this, my brother and I would look at each other in silence and nod knowingly. On cue, Dad would laugh to himself and say, 'Boys! This is the only place in the world where you can get milk from Bulls!' Once, twice, a third time, every time it was hilarious. We would laugh and laugh—not at the joke but at Dad. He was simply terrific. Another favourite joke, shamelessly stolen off him and used by Jim Jarmusch in the film *Down by Law*, referred to ice cream. 'I scream, you scream, we all scream for ice cream.' So did we!

Jewish we were, but kosher we were not. Each year I would

accompany my father to the fish and chip shop opposite parliament in Wellington to buy the first of the season's Bluff oysters. In the intervening months, we would eat pork. My mother especially liked the crackling. Years later, as she was dying, she said she would miss that more than anything—apart from her family, of course!

Funny and a little weird as he was, Dad was a smart man. He joked about life and death, but underneath all of that he was deeply serious and had figured out what really mattered in life. Someone he spoke of and admired was the Babylonian sage and scholar, Rabbi Hillel. When I was in a state, it was Hillel's famous aphorism that I remembered:

If I am not for myself, who is for me?
And when I am for myself, what am I?
And if not now, when?'

Judaism is full of these aphorisms and allegories. Scholars pore over them, arguing about their multiple meanings and the lessons that lie within. On the face of it, this is a simple one where Hillel tells us what really matters—know yourself and you will know the world; love yourself and you will be able to love others. Having found yourself, live for the benefit of others and start that now. Damn good advice, I think.

A lot of time has gone by and in the meantime the life of a jobbing junior doctor has changed enormously. No longer do they do those terrible hours, but they still work hard and the pressures on them are significant. Much cleverer than I ever was, they now compete with each other at school for top marks. They then compete again at university in the pre-med year. Now only the very best academically seem to be interviewed—so tough luck to those bus drivers out there aspiring to be doctors, you're fat out of luck.

In many countries medical students are selected directly from school, separated out from their peers and injected with increasingly addictive doses of medicine in all its fascination. At a time when their brains should be expanding out into the world, perhaps we are doing them a disservice by limiting their experiences. They are taken underground into a labyrinth of facts and figures about diseases and treatments, leaving little space and time to discover themselves and those around them.

Exhaustion and the chaos of work were some of the things that took me down so many years ago, especially responding to unexpected emergencies at all hours of the day and night. So in 1991, when I started my first specialist job 20,000 kilometres away from London, I hoped that things might be different, but they weren't. Nothing much had changed apart from me. Once again, I would regularly and frequently be called to see patients extremely late in the course of their deterioration. Some of those patients died and more were admitted to the ICU at enormous cost to themselves, their families and to the state.

At first glance, those calls seemed to come at random times of the day and night but when we looked at the data, we began to see a pattern. Most of them came at the changeover of a shift when new nurses and doctors would come on duty and see things through different eyes. When we looked at this in more detail and spent time talking to the staff, the nature of what was referred seemed to be more related to the experience, intuition and, importantly, the confidence of the nursing and medical staff on call. We also found that many staff, especially the more junior doctors and nurses, felt intimidated and scared of their seniors. This meant that they did not refer on, ask for help, or act on their intuition despite their patients so obviously not doing well.

A few years later, articles began to appear in prestigious medical journals describing the very things we were experiencing in our corner of the world. These articles detailed cases of patients clearly deteriorating over days and ultimately being unexpectedly admitted to an ICU or, worse, dying. The paper proposed a system to identify and manage those patients much earlier. Way back then a group of us tried to introduce one of those simple systems—an early warning score—into our hospital. We were too naïve and totally underestimated the barriers to implementing change despite the obvious good sense in what we were doing. It took another ten years before we gathered enough support to do this successfully and several more before it became essential everyday practice.

In the late 1990s, we intensivists also began to talk more about the changing nature of the patients we were being asked to see. Before then, our patients were generally younger people, many with infections: pneumonia in winter, infants and children with meningitis, complications of abdominal surgery and drunk people injured in car crashes or fights.

Late at night the emergency department exuded the sweet smell of alcohol and blood and under the curtains of the cubicles could be seen the blue trouser legs and black shoes of the local police. I remember one young guy who had been badly beaten outside a tavern not far from the hospital. He was brought in unconscious with obvious head injuries, fractured ribs and a collapsed lung, most likely from being kicked while he was down. He also had the worst haircut I had ever seen. The next morning, the police came to see if they could interview him but to no avail—he was still too drunk and concussed to make any sense. As they left I suggested they might wish to arrest his barber as well as those who beat him and they agreed! That's what it was like—the doctors and the police were on the same side most of the time, both in a war zone, and to stay sane we just had to see the funny side of it all.

About that time, the nature of our work started to change. Our middle of the night and early morning calls weren't to the ED to see drunks, they were to the wards, at the same ungodly hours, to see people who seemed to be suffering from the same set of diseases. Eventually we called this recurring phenomena the South Auckland Full House—a six-card hand of obesity, diabetes, renal impairment, hypertension, ischaemic heart disease and gout—a plague that is now overwhelming poor and rich nations alike.

Almost all of the patients who held the full-house hand had folders of notes recording visits to countless numbers of clinics to see doctors and nurses who looked after their different diseases and different parts of their bodies. These folders were full of reports and results, letters written by one doctor and addressed to another, always beginning with a standard format introducing the patient and outlining their previous medical problems, medications and allergies and much more. Then, and now, large swathes of each individual letter were a cut-and-paste from the previous correspondence to the next, so G-d help you if the information was wrong. The inpatient admissions were there too, detailing and documenting what seemed to be an inexorable slide toward end-stage disease. Reading this material was very helpful to understand what the medical services thought about the patient and his problems, but nowhere was there any information about the person, what they thought or, crucially, what they wanted when the wheels inevitably began to fall off.

Put yourself in my shoes. It's four in the morning and I've been asked to urgently review a patient on one of the wards. Pele is 69. He was admitted to hospital three days earlier with complications arising from his diabetes. He is now deteriorating fast. When I arrive, twelve or more members of his family—all looking extremely anxious—are gathered around him. They look at me as if I am the cavalry.

When I first started in medicine, uncertain of my own knowledge and abilities, I found situations like this incredibly confronting. Instead of acknowledging that, I felt an enormous pressure to do the opposite and bluff my way through. So, nervously, I would examine my patients, write my notes and then, feeling the gaze and expectation of the family bearing down on me, I would gabble away about all the positive things we could do to beat the disease and restore life as it once was. I felt that pressure to act so acutely, to intervene, to prescribe, to refer on for surgery, because that's what I thought I was trained to do and because that's what I thought patients and their families always wanted from us—to go all out, to prolong life in the hope that their illness and suffering would succumb to the miracle that is modern medicine.

Of course the truth is quite different from that and I now have a much better understanding of why I felt and behaved that way. Back then I was still a young man and knew little about death and dying, I completely lacked the kind of experience and confidence to help advise others staring down the barrel of their own mortality.

With the family watching my every move, I quickly introduced myself and took a look at Pele. My first impression, the end-of-the-bed-o-gram, was not good—he was pale, his breathing was irregular, he was gasping a little and his skin was yellow. When I took his hand and felt for a pulse his skin was cold.

His pulse was fast and irregular and his blood pressure was low. When I called his name he hardly stirred.

I spoke with the family to gather more information about Pele, then I asked the staff what they knew about him and, finally, I read the patient notes. The three nurses rostered on that night knew very little about him. The on-call doctor had never met him before. His medical records detailed a steady deterioration in function over the past three years, with multiple admissions to hospital for complications from his multiple illnesses. I scanned through his notes but nowhere could I find any record of a conversation with Pele and his family acknowledging that he was slowly and steadily fading away.

From my earlier position of hesitation and fear, I am now much more comfortable having these discussions. They are honest and they are meaningful and we talk about things that matter.

In the past, conversations like this—if they happened at all—were left to the junior doctors on call in the darkest hours before dawn, when people were already over the edge and falling. I knew then that it didn't have to be that way.

Informed by what I saw and learned from his notes, I sat down with the family to find out more about this man Pele, who was so clearly dying in this room in front of our eyes. There were stories and there were tears and, in the end, there was relief in the faces of this family, who knew him better than anybody and had seen his progressive deterioration over many months. Of course we will care for him, I told them, but our attention and efforts will focus on his comfort, not on trying to save his life—he had been beyond that for months.

In my years as a specialist, I have had hundreds of conversations like this, all of them with families wanting the best for the person they love. Outside of the intensive care unit, when I see new patients like Pele, I work hard to establish an immediate rapport with them. In my experience that is best done by being polite, respectful and honest; by listening to the patient and their family; by showing a genuine interest in the person and not just their illness; by acknowledging what you don't know and, importantly, by doing what you say you will do. Open-ended questions can be enormously helpful in finding out what they know, what they fear and what they hope for. 'What do you understand is going on with your mum?', 'What do you think she would want for herself?' are simple examples. Conducted well, these discussions will usually deliver answers to the difficult questions and a way forward will emerge. This means that what could have been a contentious and tricky situation is resolved to the tangible relief and benefit of all involved.

Inside the intensive care unit, I will never walk past a family visiting one of our patients without stopping to say hello and to chat. That, combined with our open visiting policy for family and friends, means they see us at work, with each other, with other patients and their families. As we chat among ourselves, they also get a sense of who we are as people outside of being a doctor or a nurse. So when it comes to more formal discussions about difficult decisions, we already have a relationship together, which eases the process for all of us.

Those more formal meetings serve multiple purposes for all parties. They allow us to ensure that the families have all the information they need to understand what has happened to their loved one. They provide families with the opportunity to ask questions, and for them to play a meaningful role in the decision making that will ultimately follow. These meetings are also a chance for the medical staff to be clear about our role in taking responsibility for those decisions. By way of example I have not and will never ask a family to make the call to remove someone they love from a ventilator—that decision is a medical one. At the same time I would never remove a patient from the ventilator if the family objected.

My approach is to engage families and to always take them with me as we work through those difficult decisions, ensuring that they understand all that they need to understand, and, in the end, accept our plan.

Compassion and patience helps people on this journey to come to understand that the one they love is beyond our help and to agree with our plan to return them to a more natural state or put them in the hands of G-d. This takes time because individual family members come to accept the seemingly unacceptable in their own time. Occasionally, I hear about a stand-off between a group of doctors and a family unable to agree on a proposed management plan, but in all my years in practice that has never happened to me.

Years have passed and so much has changed in how we think about, plan and deliver health services. Patients and their families are now much more at the centre of what we do and more involved than ever in contributing to their own health plans. Services are increasingly being devolved to where patients live, in their communities, and close to where they work. Our junior doctors are increasingly unburdened by fewer hours at work. Our hospitals have adopted early warning scores and we are detecting and intervening earlier to improve the outcomes for acutely unwell patients with unstable physiology. All these things are good and contribute to improving the value of our investment in health, the most costly sector of government spending, but we are still a long way from where we ought to be—a nation of people who are independent, self-reliant, healthy and well.

My best ever patient –

72154

My mother had many different names. Zosia was her birth name, but that became anglicised to Sophie by her New Zealand friends. My father called her Stara, Polish for old or more colloquially 'old girl'. I called her 'Ma' when I was small and 'Zaza' later in life, because that's what my kids called her. In the fifteen years before she died, that was shortened to 'Z'. Records kept by others remember her as a number—72154. It was tattooed on her left forearm, the seven written in the European style with a stroke across it. I have always written my sevens the same way. She answered to all those names but never to the number.

Zaza was born on 3 May 1929, the only child of Hilary Minc and Cecilia Kronenblum. She remembered growing up in a large modern apartment in the Polish town of Katowice, not so far from the border with Germany. Hers was a very wealthy family and before the war they lived a beautiful life.

Hilary worked for Cecilia's father, who owned a large iron foundry, Fabryke Odelwow Zelaznych-I-Kaklady Mechaniczne S. Kronenblum, in nearby Konskie. There they manufactured the ovens that were so popular in many Polish homes at the time. My mother remembered Hilary as a devoted father who spent a lot of time with her in the parks and cafes, where he always read her stories.

As for her mother Cecilia, Zaza remembered her as a beautiful woman with flaming auburn hair, quite like my daughter's now. Always surrounded by friends, she loved the high life, parties, balls, and riding horses. She was 26 when her daughter was born and not terribly motherly, something my mother resented at the time but later, given what happened, she was pleased that Cecilia had the chance to have such fun.

Zaza arrived in New Zealand on board a Catalina on the overnight flight from Sydney, landing softly on the water at Evans Bay. It was the last leg of a very long journey from Tel Aviv where she and my father married three months before; he was forty, she was 22. Returning to the country that adopted him after the end of the war, ever the romantic, Dad was there with flowers to meet her.

Despite their devotion to each other, life in New Zealand was not easy for his young bride. She had lived a life no one should experience. She spoke with a thick Polish accent, had little English, and everywhere she went, people stared at her. Z was different. She had a tattoo on her arm, she ate different food, she dressed differently, and she missed the life she had had in Tel Aviv.

Like her mother, Zaza was beautiful, and loved people and a good party. In company she was gracious and funny. People flocked to her. Ironically, it was these very differences that attracted people to her. Wherever she went she became the centre of attention but behind all of that was a past that would always haunt her and an ever-present anxiety about what might happen in the future.

In Poland, soon after the war, she was told not to try to have children, but she did. All the way through her pregnancies, first with my brother Les and then with me, she was afraid that her babies would die in utero or be deformed. Twice, her joy at giving birth to a normal child was tinged with the guilt that only survivors know. 'How can I be so lucky? Why did I survive? What did I do? Did I collaborate? Give in? Turn someone in? Take someone's place?' This was how she thought.

I knew we were different too. Different like the Hiltons, the Weiss family, Marisha and Manek, Wizcek and Lala, and the rest of the madcap Wellington Jewish community from eastern Europe, who were defined by their experiences of the war and their displacement to this far corner of the world.

Yes, I was like them but I didn't want to be. I wanted to be a normal kid like the ones at school with their bird cutter hair, shaved sides and fluffy top knots, and jam sandwiches for lunch. For a few years at primary school, I was embarrassed to bring my friends home to meet my mother because of the way she spoke and because I was scared that she might offer them an ox tongue sandwich, a bowl of sauerkraut or a Polish sausage. I was young and just trying to fit in. I had no idea of what my mother had really suffered. I think that was the way my parents wanted it too—them and us just fitting in. My parents never spoke Polish, German or Hebrew around us, always English. We were called David and Leslie. Mum was happy to be called Sophie, and my father even allowed some of his acquaintances to call him Tony!

Especially at the beginning, they worked hard to leave the past behind them. It became a foreign country where they no longer went.

My early memories of my father were of him at our kitchen

table, with pen and paper, later with an old typewriter and always with wads of documents and notes. Later, I understood that this was my dad-the-lawyer making a claim against the German government for compensation for my mother's suffering and losses during the war. Each letter, carefully composed in German, some occasionally in English, was copied on carbon paper and then stored in chronological order. Every month, sometimes more frequently, a reply would arrive addressed to Mrs Zosia Galler, PO Box 1538, Wellington, New Zealand, and then the cycle would repeat.

This correspondence recorded my father's interviews with my mother, a reluctant participant at first, detailing the individual horrors that befell her and her family during those dreadful years. Witnessing the execution of her father, the transport to Auschwitz, the terrible stories from that journey, my mother and Cecilia's first encounter with the 'Angel of Death' Josef Mengele, and much more.

Each claim required verification so my mother was regularly required to speak to officials from the German embassy, to see a psychiatrist, to remember things that no nine year old could possibly remember. The process was gruelling and it was prolonged, but it was, in the end at least, a bit therapeutic. Perhaps without knowing it, in doing what he did, I am convinced my father saved my mother's sanity. Dragged into these conversations, she was at last able to speak about some of those ghastly experiences, releasing a bit of the pain.

This correspondence, at first with the German government directly, then through a lawyer in Wiesbaden, started in 1954 and concluded in 1965. Finally my mother was awarded a pension for life, a monthly sum paid in Deutsche Marks. My father explained this injection of foreign funds as something that afforded us a new car every time the ashtrays were full. My mother was a chain smoker so there were a lot of them.

While I knew what Dad was doing all those evenings at the kitchen table, the Holocaust and Auschwitz were just words to me. I had no idea of what they really meant until years later. I must have been a teenager near the end of my high school years and at home with my parents one evening we watched a television series about the Second World War that showed the liberation of the Auschwitz concentration camp.

I have no idea whether my mother knew what was coming but as the images of death and horror were playing on the television screen, she let out a cry that I will never forget. She then began to sob in a way that shocked me like nothing since. Dad turned the television off and tried to comfort her but nothing worked. She cried and cried and then fell mute with a look of complete exhaustion on her face. Soon after, our GP arrived, rolled up her sleeve and gave her an injection and Dad put her to bed. I was stunned by all of this, my mother's grief, my father's immersion in what was happening to Mum, and how oblivious they both were to the presence of me and my brother.

In the ghetto, then in the camp my mother was in a state of constant starvation and suffered from recurrent bouts of disease, especially dysentery and typhoid. Still a child, she learned to be tough and not display any signs of weakness because if you did you would never be seen again. Such a fate befell her mother, the beautiful Cecilia. Exhausted and fading away, she developed frostbite in her foot. As infection took hold, she became even weaker and, despite help from her ten-year-old daughter, collapsed at the morning roll call. She was beaten with a lash but could still not stand. Cecilia was then bundled up and taken to the 'hospital' where her foot was amputated without anaesthetic.

She died soon after. In her memoir, Zaza remembered that she never cried after the death of her mother. In fact, she said she felt a sense of relief because from then on she only had to look out for herself. Perhaps that's why, towards the end of her life, it was her mother whom she wanted to remember and talk about.

There was so much more like that, endless acts of indescribable cruelty, occasional acts of kindness, but in that place it was survival of the fittest and my mother learned how to survive. When the war was over and after the United Nations Refugee Association moved her from an orphanage in Poland to Palestine, she slipped into a new life. She did this again when she arrived in New Zealand, but wherever she went she could not escape the physical and emotional impact of what she had lived through. To my knowledge, Zaza never had a breakdown like that again. However, her traumatic past never left her in peace and continued to play out in different ways, even coming back to haunt her in the hours before her death.

My mother always kept the bedroom lights on at night and she slept badly. When she did manage to sleep, it was always accompanied by the same set of nightmares. Nothing seemed to make them go away, not even the sleeping pills; initially one, then two, then more. Instead, she learned to live with the nightmares as she did with many of the other torments she suffered.

For years I encouraged her to seek help from a psychologist but she always refused. In the end she did what she always did—she adapted to the situation she found herself in, almost as though she could live her new life in parallel with the torments of the past put temporarily aside.

A proud and elegant woman, a few years after I was born my mother began to gain weight. She grew increasingly tired and constantly complained that she was cold. When she combed her hair tufts would come away from her scalp. The same seemed to be happening to her eyebrows, which were thinning progressively and almost disappearing at their ends. When she looked in the mirror, her face was fat. With all of this came an intellectual lethargy that my father thought was depression. Talking to him later, he recalled one doctor suggesting she go into a mental hospital for ECT, but Dad refused. He knew there was another cause for what was happening to her and he eventually found it in the rooms of a well-known physician in Wellington. As soon as he saw her he knew immediately. My mother had the classic appearance of someone suffering from a lack of the thyroid hormone thyroxine—the thinning hair, the loss of the lateral part of the eyebrows, the dull waxy skin, the history of cold intolerance, and the weight gain. She was a textbook case. There is a German word, schadenfreude, which describes much about doctors—in essence it means getting pleasure from someone else's misfortune. My bet is that the physician concerned will have taken almost as much pleasure in seeing such a textbook case of hypothyroidism as he would have in curing it.

Being the thorough physician that he was, he would have done a series of other investigations to determine why her thyroid gland had ceased to function. He would also have checked whether she had become pre-diabetic and had a high level of cholesterol in her blood. He started her off on replacement therapy pills that she took for the rest of her life.

Over the following week, the cloud lifted and my mother began to emerge. A month later, she started to look like she used to. Her hair was back, her eyebrows had grown and she was returning to her normal weight. It was a miracle and my dad was over the moon.

A few years later, when I was about seven, I came home from school one day to find my mother collapsed on the kitchen floor surrounded by blood. I rang my dad and he phoned our GP. A refugee like them, he suggested giving Mum bread to eat. An odd response but even then I knew he was more interested in golf than he was in medicine. Soon after, an ambulance arrived and Mum was rushed to hospital. That night she had emergency surgery for what turned out to be a bleeding ulcer that had eroded into a big vessel in the lining of her stomach.

During the operation, known as a Billroth I procedure, the surgeon removed the lower part of her stomach where the ulcer was, joining the remnant directly to the first part of the small bowel. From then on, Mum was only able to eat very small amounts at any sitting. She also began to suffer from a burning pain caused by the reflux of stomach acid into the oesophagus, a condition that most likely caused the cancer that killed her so many years later.

Her beauty restored, and well recovered from her operation, Zaza continued her adaptation to life in New Zealand. She was a terrible cook but still loved to entertain. Most Sundays we had people to lunch.

On one occasion, one of Mum's girlfriends came with her new husband, a German baron! Other friends, Manek and Marisa, were there too. Things were going well. Mum cooked meatballs and sauerkraut. The adults were drinking wine and the conversation was flowing until my mother asked a few questions of the baron, obviously a wealthy and successful man. It turned out he was part of the famous Krupps family, now having moved their interests from munitions into coffee machines and the like.

'Ahhhh, Krupps. I used to work for them,' my mother said.

'Where?' asked the baron.

'Auschwitz,' my mother replied with a snarl.

Things at the table went quiet for a while, then to put people at ease Mum told a story from the time when she arrived in Palestine after the war.

She recalled how surprised she was that most of the cars were Mercedes Benz. When she asked why, after all the terrible things the Germans had done to the Jews, her friend held up his arms and shrugged in the way that only we Jews can and said, 'Because they are very good cars.'

Years later I owned a fabulous pumpkin-coloured Mercedes 280SE. I loved it and so did my mother!

After those early encounters with medical services, Zaza spent the rest of her life avoiding doctors apart from the time spent with me and my brother, the best intensive care doctor in New Zealand. But as proud of us as she was, we had little influence over her in matters medical. Her smoking was a case in point. This was something she started in Auschwitz and continued until only a day or two before she died. She was convinced that smoking had helped keep her alive then and that she would be immune from its harmful effects now. In many ways she was a fatalist. When we talked about why she had survived, she simply attributed it to luck and that seemed to be the philosophy that guided her later in life. What will be will be, that's what she believed, and that's how she lived.

Although my parents loved life in New Zealand, there were a few occasions when they were made to feel unwelcome and sometimes afraid. One of those was after the publication of an interview with my mother where she spoke about her experiences in the war. Soon after that our car was daubed with a swastika and my mother received phone calls threatening her life. This was terrifying and put her on edge for years, effectively stopping her from engaging in any public discourse about her past for a very long time, and denying her those opportunities to steadily heal the scars of the past.

My partner Ema and my mother had a very special relationship in the way that only women can. They adored each other and confided in each other, so if ever my mother was to tell her story to anyone, it would be to Ema.

Overcoming her reluctance, my mother finally agreed to record her story to ensure that her children and grandchildren and those who come after them have a record not only of her experiences, but of the lives and the fates of her parents and grandparents. Those conversations took place over several weeks and were recorded then subsequently transcribed. Together with the correspondence between my father and the German government, they formed the basis for *As It Was*, my mother's memoir, published privately in 2005.

Two years before she died, she agreed to record a video interview that is now shown to school parties and visitors to Wellington's Holocaust Centre. Soon after doing this she began to receive letters of thanks and bunches of flowers from members of the various school parties who visited the centre. These were a fabulous surprise for my mother and reinforced how right she was to finally share her story.

In January 1945, as Soviet forces closed in on occupied Poland, those prisoners at Auschwitz that could walk were rounded up and marched north towards the labour camps in Germany in what is now known as the 'Death March'. Those who could not walk were executed. It was a brutal affair, months on foot, in the bitter cold with little food.

After just weeks, of the 3600 that left Auschwitz, only 800 were still alive—and then only just. Almost at the point of complete exhaustion, recognising that time was running out, a girl of a similar age who had befriended my mother helped her escape.

Years later, on the day of my father's funeral, my mother received a letter from a friend in Sydney. Enclosed with it was a short article from one of the Australian papers written by a woman who was looking for the girl that escaped with her from the Death March. Our Sydney friends thought that this could be Zosia. They were right.

The timing of this letter was bizarre. It was both deeply disturbing as well as potentially wonderful news. A few weeks later, when she was able, my mother replied but didn't receive a response for several months. When it came it was a relatively formal response written on behalf of the woman to inform us that she was now in psychiatric care following the suicide of her son, who also had trained as a doctor. Weeks later, the response to my mother's reply was to inform her that her Death March companion was also now dead, she too having committed suicide.

Much has been written about the psychological fate of survivors and how the suffering of one generation impacts on the next. Until then I had studiously avoided thinking about that because it was too hard for me. Instead, I remained in a state of denial, consumed by my own life, unwilling and unable to confront the horror of what happened to my mother. In the end, I was helped to do that by spending much more time with her, and by Ema, who did what I could never have done—record my mother's story.

Because of work commitments, between 2003 and 2010, I spent every second week with my mother in Wellington. Over that time I got to know and understand her better. As a mature adult, it was not an experience I would have expected, but it turned into an interesting and fabulous time for both of us.

We had a lot of fun apart from a few too many phone calls from her wondering where I was. What time would I be home? Was I all right? What did I want for dinner? We enjoyed each other's company.

She was an extraordinary role model in so many ways. Having suffered so much, you might think that my mother would be full of hatred and bitterness, especially toward the Germans. She wasn't.

Although she could never forgive them for what happened, and despite the tyranny of memories replayed every night when she slept, somehow she turned what could have been a deeply destructive force into one for good. She was generous and she was kind. She loved people and hearing their stories, and she was a friend you could confide in. Her circle included mainly women of her age, but also friends of mine. They loved her and she loved them. She was open-minded, smart and, if bothered, politically savvy too. Unlike so many of her generation, she was not easily fooled by a false smile and the superficial promises of inarticulate politicians. Unusually, my mother seemed to become more liberal as she got older.

But by the end of my stint with her, she was beginning to lose weight, eat less and smoke more. Her friends cajoled her, convinced that she didn't eat at all when she was alone. Thankfully that was a rare event because the house was always full of people. She loved the company but at the same time the constant round of visitors started to exhaust her.

Over the next year she managed surprisingly well. She took several road trips with friends and spent time in the warmth somewhere north of Brisbane. We were so used to her chewing

Quick-Eze and swallowing her usual pills that maybe we were a bit slow to notice the increasing discomfort she was feeling in her upper abdomen. When we did, we suggested that it might be a good time to see a doctor. When she immediately agreed, we knew something was seriously wrong.

Mum didn't like going to doctors and hadn't seen one in years. She hardly ever had her thyroid hormone levels measured and learned with help from her doctor sons how to adjust her dose according to how she felt. It was always obvious to me when her levels were too high, because her anxiety levels would go through the roof and her heart would race.

My mother used to say, 'Doctors, why would I go see them, they'll just tell me I've got cancer.' What she didn't know wouldn't hurt her, that's what she thought. Although she said it as a joke, it wasn't. It was her fear and anxiety speaking, the same fear and anxiety that had plagued her her entire life.

In mid-February 2012, my mother finally went to see the doctor she vowed never to see. To add insult to injury, he referred her to another one, a gastroenterologist. He asked her lots of questions and then examined her thoroughly. His fears were ours. My mother's history of weight loss, reflux and now quite severe pain in her upper abdomen whenever she ate were ominous signs that would be consistent with a cancer of the oesophagus or stomach.

The next day she went in for an upper gastrointestinal endoscopy, a simple procedure performed under light sedation, where a narrow tube with a camera on its end is passed into the mouth and down through the oesophagus into the stomach and then into the first part of the duodenum. As he did this the cause of her pain and weight loss became obvious—a large, ugly area at the junction of the upper stomach and lower oesophagus, most likely a cancer. He took biopsies, withdrew the scope, and waited for my mother to wake up.

She couldn't remember exactly what the doctor told her after the procedure, but my mother was clear that he was worried about something and that we needed to wait for the results of the biopsies.

In the meantime, we did our best to stay measured and take things bit by bit. At first glance you would have thought that nothing had changed. Mum smoked. She had her usual few glasses of wine in the evening and, when we were with her, she even ate quite well. Maybe, just maybe, she would be okay?

Sadly, that turned out to be wishful thinking. Sometimes when you see someone every day you don't always notice small changes in how they look or behave. You want to see what you want to see. That was me until that moment when the results finally arrived—adenocarcinoma of the oesophagus.

Mum wasn't surprised, it was what she had expected. This was her fate. Suddenly, she looked frail and thin, her skin looked more sallow, her hair seemed to have lost its lustre and she had a worried look on her face.

Later that night, we shared a few glasses of wine and joked. 'What a bugger,' I said, 'you were right all along about those doctors.'

She laughed and I laughed—but neither of us really thought it was that funny.

The next day, my brother Les came down from Auckland and that evening the three of us, my mother and her two sons, the intensive care specialists, sat together around the kitchen table for the conversation we all needed to have.

In many ways it was like any other family gathering. There was wine, a plate of my mother's divine chicken and spinach crepes, and a big salad on the table; but this was going to be a different evening. Zaza seemed to have prepared herself for this judging by the look on her face. It was one I had seen before—a look of steely determination, a sign of her readiness to confront what lay ahead.

We began to talk. Carcinoma of the oesophagus is usually a highly lethal disease with a five-year survival of about 10 per cent. Putting that another way, if we were to take 100 patients with the disease, after five years of treatment about ninety would have died and ten might still be alive. Could she be one of the ten? That was one of the first things we talked about.

Blood tests and a CT scan to stage the tumour might help answer that, but whatever they showed, the treatment options—surgery or chemotherapy—would be brutal and likely destroy the quality of what time she had left or, at worst, would hasten her death.

Zaza was pulling faces. She knew the score. She was 82 and already frail. She was clear that surgery and other aggressive and likely futile treatments to extend her life were things that she didn't want and, in my heart, I already knew this was going to be the ultimate test of 'less is more'.

I have had hundreds of meetings with individuals and families facing difficult decisions. They have taught me how to behave, how to listen, and how to gently engage complete strangers in conversations about living and dying, about loss and grief, and most importantly about what matters to them at the end.

There is no turning the clock back and pretending nothing has changed, so when life is turned on its head, as it was for my mother, our only option was to do what we could to make the most of the situation we were in. To say that I have enjoyed those conversations is probably not the best way to describe how I feel when they have gone well. It's more a feeling of having done the right thing, to reach a point where my patients and their families understand their position and feel empowered to make the most of it. These were the thoughts filling my head as we talked with Mum.

Sitting there at the kitchen table, it was as though she could read my mind. Before we could specifically ask, she began to talk about the things that really mattered to her. She wanted to know how much time she had left. We said that no one could be sure but probably no more than a few months. She asked whether she would be in a lot of pain as the tumour progressed. We weren't sure of that either but promised that if she had pain, we would manage that with expert help and make sure she was comfortable. Finally, we got to the hardest thing for her to ask—for our time and our company, for her not to be alone when she needed us. You might think that's strange but it's not.

Years before, when my father was becoming increasingly unwell in the months before his death, he steadily prepared my mother for a life without him. Up to that point, he had managed everything in his quiet and caring way, apart of course from their social lives. He did all the odd jobs and practical things that we take for granted but without which the ship would sink—the bills, the finances and investments, the driving, and so much more.

Two months before he died, after 37 driving lessons, my mother finally got her first driver's licence. Dad even bought her a small car—a Daihatsu Charade, which she crashed on her first outing. Repaired, it sat in her garage for the next 22 years, driven only by my brother and me when we came to town. After Mum died we gave it to her gardener.

Looking back, what Dad was doing was obvious, but silly self-indulgent me, I didn't get it. He had slowly helped Zaza become comfortable with making decisions that she had never had to make before, at the same time as teaching her a set of principles to help when he was gone. One of those was to live within her means, Dad's shorthand for not spending the capital and learning to live off the interest—an analogy that extended beyond sound financial management to her not living in her children's pockets and consciously allowing them to live their own lives. That was the reason why Mum was so reluctant to ask for our time.

There we were, the three of us, at the end of the evening, full of crepes and wine, happy that we had found our way together. It was clear—we would make the best of the time that Mum had left. There would be no interventions to stop what we couldn't stop. Instead, our efforts would be focused on keeping Zaza at home, ensuring her comfort, and for us to be with her when she needed us.

The next day that was put to the test with the arrival of an invitation to visit the surgical outpatient clinic at the nearby hospital the following week. Prior to attending the appointment, Mum was required to have several panels of blood tests and a CT scan of her chest and abdomen.

The surgical clinic was in one of those typically dilapidated old buildings that used to be part of an old hospital now rebuilt. We arrived on time to a near-empty waiting room manned by a smiling receptionist. It's fair to say that, despite being clear about our position and what we wanted, Mum and I were both incredibly nervous, but about what it's hard to say now.

After twenty minutes or so, we were shown into the consultant surgeon's rooms. He was a young and handsome man, born in India and trained in the UK and New Zealand. In front of him, he had a set of notes and letters. He was apologetic because they didn't seem to contain the results of the blood tests and the CT scan that he had ordered. We tried to put him at ease, telling him that we hadn't thought those necessary. However, before we had the chance to explain why, he became irritated and cross. It was then that my mother spoke up, explaining what she understood about her condition and why she had decided not to proceed with the tests. As she spoke, we saw the surgeon lighten up, his head nodding as my mother explained her position. I knew immediately that he would be feeling the same sense of relief as I so often have in the past when speaking with patients who knew what they wanted, especially when you knew they were right. This young man was off the hook, no smoke and mirrors here. I sat back and listened to them talk about life, about death and even about reincarnation! It was very moving.

Having got that out of the way, the two of us then went to see the GP that Mum never really saw. He was thrilled to finally meet my mother and genuinely distressed by what she was going through. Through him, we made contact with the local hospice and with their help documented my mother's wishes with the ambulance service and the local hospital. We also put in place an alert that should the paramedics be called to treat my mother in the event of an emergency, they would immediately contact the hospice nurses and those nurses would then call me. What an incredibly smart move that turned out to be.

Over the next two months, life for me returned to normal. Zaza did well too, living on her own as she had been for so long, but now with a small group of her closest friends looking after her. They spoke with her each morning, rang her regularly, and took her out on jaunts and shopping trips. They were a terrific group of women who knew what my mother wanted and, importantly, they also had the key to Mum's house.

Zaza and I spoke on the phone at least twice a day, and my brother and I took turns to visit her every week. Each time she looked more frail, but remained as engaging and hospitable as ever. Wine glass in one hand, cigarette in the other, she would roll her eyes and repeat her only complaint, 'Who said old age was golden?'

We spoke about all sorts of things, and from time to time we even talked about her dying—it was not an easy topic to discuss. I had mistakenly thought that because Mum had seen so much death in her life that she was not afraid of dying herself. I was wrong. Auschwitz was no hospice. There death was never peaceful. It was not the final act of a life well lived. There it was a process of torment, of loss and grief, feelings of hopelessness and immense suffering. There men, women and children were dragged from their lives and slaughtered.

It finally dawned on me: it was not death itself that terrified my mother, it was the process of dying. She was a 'survivor' and it seemed now there was no surviving this. As simple as that might sound, this was a light-bulb moment for both of us, because I felt confident that we could control that process with medications to protect her from what she feared.

One afternoon, not long after my last visit, she didn't answer the phone when I rang. I waited for another five minutes and rang again. I tried to suppress the anxiety welling up in me, telling myself that she was probably out with her friends. Finally, I rang one of them, Barbara. She had seen Zaza that morning and said she was tired but otherwise well, and wondered if she might be sleeping. Mum never slept through a phone call and before I could ask, Barbara offered to call by the house and ring me back.

I don't know what it was but I was convinced that something bad had happened so I quickly packed a bag. When Barbara rang back, all that was confirmed. Mum had fallen down her stairs. She was covered in blood and barely conscious. The ambulance was on its way.

As I arrived at the airport in Auckland, one of the hospice nurses rang to tell me more. Most likely she'd had a stroke, causing her to fall, because Mum had difficulty speaking and wasn't moving her right arm and leg. She also seemed to be in pain, the nurse thought from broken ribs and the wounds on her arms and legs, where the skin had sheared away.

Hospice nurses are special. They are smart, experienced, compassionate and kind, but they are also deeply practical too. I told them that I was only an hour away and asked their advice. 'You know what my mother wanted, between us, can we be true to that?'

When I finally arrived at Zaza's place, she was already upstairs in bed, carried there by burly men from the local fire brigade. She would have enjoyed that. Two nurses were washing and dressing her wounds. The nurses had given her a small dose of morphine and she appeared comfortable. Her facial droop obvious, Mum gave me a sideways glance of recognition but didn't speak.

After a couple hours, when they were done, we formulated the first of our many plans. We started with what we were going to do tonight, or to be more accurate, what I was going to do that first night to look after Mum.

It was only later, when I was alone with her, that the enormity of what I had taken on hit me. It wasn't that together we didn't know what to do; we did. What I felt was a mix of terror at the overwhelming sense of responsibility and commitment to do this for *my mother* but, at the same time, knowing that it was something I really wanted to do for her as well as for me.

Over the next few days, we got into a groove. It started with a visit from a lovely palliative care specialist who I immediately warmed to. He came with the same two hospice nurses and spoke directly to Mum. She acknowledged him with a few mumbled words. We talked about the services they offered, how we would manage pain and any side effects of the medications. He told us about the equipment we could borrow to get Zaza out of bed, to the loo and into a chair. We also found out about other community resources that would send people to come and wash and bathe my mother every day.

Later that day, Ema came down from Auckland. A few days later, my brother arrived too, and then his wife. Quite quickly, as a family, we formulated a roster to give each of us time to spend with Mum and also time for breaks. As terrible as the situation was, we warmed to our task. We were together as a family and as a result became closer than we ever had been before.

I was staggered at how well Mum did. It wasn't long before she was able to speak more coherently and, with a lot of help, get into a chair to spend a few hours in the sun overlooking her small garden. She smoked and drank wine left-handed now. In her dark glasses, she looked every bit the ageing movie star. This was a special time that I will always treasure.

Those terrific days went on for just over a week before she began to fade. Like a bubble floating higher and higher then steadily dropping toward earth, Mum became increasingly tired and less able to do things for herself. No more trips to the chair at the bedroom window. We held the cigarettes and wine glass to her mouth now, her physical strength ebbing away fast. She was on a concoction of medicines too—one to keep her comfortable, another to ward off nausea, a third to help with her breathing.

Never her strongest suit, Zaza first stopped eating. Next, she stopped drinking, showing no interest in her evening glass of wine. Then her speech became harder to understand except, of course, when it came to knowing when she wanted another cigarette.

Before too long she drifted into a steady sleep, snoring quietly when she was flat on her back. She had a presence, my mother, powerful in life and now, so close to death, still there. Days passed and nothing changed until that terrible Friday morning of 8 June.

Suddenly and unexpectedly, she sat up in bed with a look of abject terror on her face, crying and screaming just like she had in front of the television so many years ago. Here we were, sixty years later and thousands of miles away at the edge of the world, and still the horror of her childhood came back to haunt her one last time. I was there with Ema and Les. We were distraught and did all we could to comfort her, Ema cradling Mum's head in her arms, her doctor sons hopelessly out of their depth, all of us just wanting to get her to sleep.

At this point, Mum's medications were being steadily injected under her skin but the doses were small and, we realised at that time, totally inadequate for what she was suffering now. We responded by increasing her dose but it was another twenty minutes before she finally drifted back to sleep, this time with a more peaceful look on her face. Later that night, she quietly stopped breathing, a smile on her face, in her own home, free at last.

Desperately sad, but at the same time relieved, we sat with her not quite knowing what to do. I called Jo, a close friend steeped in Jewish tradition. She came by and we did what Jews do when someone dies. I can hardly remember what it was now but it didn't take long and when we were done, the three of us felt a lot better. Jo left and we hit the whiskey.

The next day Zaza left in a black car, to return home two days later for the last time. She looked good, like she was asleep, so different from what I saw when I visited my father in a funeral home so many years before. There he had a look on his face that I had never seen before; it upset me enormously then and still does today.

To the surprise of many, my mother's funeral did not take place in a synagogue—'I never go to a synagogue now, why would I want to go to one when I'm dead?' she used to say. Instead it was at St Andrew's, an inner-city church on the Terrace in Wellington, a fine place known for its tolerance. It was a moving and fabulous affair, followed by a good party in the Wellesley Club, where she had celebrated her eightieth birthday.

For the next few weekends, Ema and I flew down to Wellington to do what most children do when their parents die—go through their affairs and possessions. We started in the pantry with its bowing shelves, loaded with cans of the mundane and the exotic, most well past their use-by dates. There was enough there to feed an army or withstand a long siege. This hoarding was another manifestation of my mother's post-holocaust mindset. There were cupboards full of photographs of us as kids, friends of my parents now long dead, Mum and Dad on holiday. There were drawers full of trinkets and costume jewellery acquired throughout the entire period of my parents' marriage. There were also rooms full of clothes to be gone through. We packed bag after bag; most went to the Salvation Army, some terrific things to the Hospice shop, but most went to the local landfill. Mum would not have minded that. Her early childhood was spent in relative opulence before all that was lost and, after much suffering, found again in the long loving relationship she had with my father. By then, material things meant little to her; it was human contact and the warmth of her friendships that mattered.

In accordance with my mother's wishes she was cremated, not buried, as she should have been according to Jewish lore—but about this she had always been resolute. She wanted to go the same way as her mother, whose body was burnt in the ovens of Auschwitz.

Two years later Les, Ema and I made the journey south and finally did what we promised to do—interred her ashes in my father's grave at the cemetery she hated to visit, at Makara, near the sea on the south coast of their city.

I feel lucky and I feel privileged to have had the chance to spend so much time with my mother, my best ever patient; to look after her when she fell ill, to understand what mattered to her and, in the end, to be with her when she needed me. Now a few years down the line, I still miss her terribly but looking back on our relationship, I have no regrets. Maybe that's as good as it gets.

ACKNOWLEDGEMENTS

Thank you for all that you have taught me; how every day, you have inspired me with your resilience, courage and humanity. Without you I would have given up long ago.

My ongoing gratitude to my family for their unending patience, good humour and critique.

And a special note of thanks to my publisher for giving me the opportunity to sit still and write this short memoir.

GLOSSARY

Adenocarcinoma of the oesophagus: a cancer that starts in the gland cells that make mucus in the lining of the oesophagus. Adenocarcinomas are found mainly in the lower third of the oesophagus. This type of cancer is most associated with acid reflux.

Anaemia: a deficiency of red cells in the blood

Aneurysm: an abnormal weakness in the wall of an artery. When they rupture in the arterial circulation of the brain they can cause a stroke that can be fatal. In the thoracic aorta, aneurysms can be associated with inherited conditions like Marfan's syndrome and with hypertension. Aneurysms in the abdominal aorta are often associated with smoking.

Angina (also known as angina pectoris): chest pain caused by lack of oxygen flow to the heart

Apnoea: a sleep condition where no breathing occurs for short periods

Asystole (also known as 'flatlining'): when the heart shows no electrical activity and ceases to pump blood

Autosomal dominant: a gene mutation that can be passed on by only one parent

Bacterial endocarditis: a bacterial infection that affects the heart valves, most commonly those on the left side of the heart—the mitral and aortic valves. Associated with the deposition of infective material on the valves themselves, which are commonly referred to as vegetations.

Body Mass Index (BMI): a measure of weight adjusted for height, calculated by dividing your weight in kilograms by your height in metres squared (kg/m^2)

Bolus: administration of a small amount of a drug

Bilirubin: a substance created by the breakdown of red blood cells; it is usually excreted by the liver

Bronchiolitis: inflammation of the small airways in the lungs caused by a viral infection most commonly occurring in infants

Bubble CPAP (Continuous positive airway pressure): a non-invasive system that assists new-born babies to breathe

Cardiac arrest: a sudden stop in circulation and the forward flow of blood out of the heart to the body, caused by ventricular fibrillation—an abnormal rhythm of the heart—or asystole, when there is no electrical activity in the heart and therefore no muscle contraction

Cardioplegia: a solution administered to stop the heart during surgery

Cellulitis: a bacterial infection of the skin and the tissues beneath the skin

Cholera: a bacterial infection of the small intestine that causes severe diarrhoea

Cholecystitis: an inflammation of the gallbladder usually because of an obstruction to the flow of bile, caused by a gallstone

Creatinine: a by-product of muscle metabolism that is usually removed from the body by the kidneys

CT (computerised tomography) scan: numerous X-ray images combined to create a full picture of the scanned object

Dialysis: a life-support treatment that uses a machine to filter harmful wastes, salt, and excess fluid from blood, thereby restoring it to a healthy balance. Dialysis replaces many of the kidney's important functions.

Directed donation: when friends or relatives donate blood, an organ or tissue to a specified intended recipient

Electrocardiogram (ECG): a test that measures the electrical activity of the heart over a period of time

Epiglottitis: an inflammation of the epiglottis

Gelfoam: an absorbable gelatine powder used to stem bleeding

Glasgow Coma Scale: a scale which physicians use to measure a patient's level of consciousness

Glomerulus: part of the nephron in the kidney; this cluster of capillaries is where blood is initially filtered removing plasma, water, electrolytes, proteins and waste products

Heart attack (also known as myocardial infarction): caused by a blockage in the flow of oxygenated blood within the coronary arteries that supply the heart. A heart attack is usually signalled by chest pain, profuse sweating, sometimes nausea and a heavy crushing pain in the chest. This pain can also radiate to the left shoulder and arm. A heart attack can lead to an abnormal heart rhythm and result in a cardiac arrest.

HELLP syndrome: a condition in pregnancy related to pre-eclampsia, whose name is an acronym of its three main features: haemolysis, elevated liver enzymes, and low platelet count

Homeostasis: a term to describe the property of a system in which variables are regulated so that internal conditions remain stable and relatively constant

Hyperglycaemia: abnormally high level of glucose in the blood

Hypertrophy: Cardiac hypertrophy is a thickening of the heart muscle (myocardium) which results in a decrease in size of the chamber of the heart, including the left and right ventricles. A common cause of cardiac hypertrophy is high blood pressure (hypertension) and heart valve stenosis.

Hypoxaemia: abnormally low levels of oxygen in the blood

Internal jugular vein: drains blood from the brain, face, and neck. Two of these veins lie along each side of the neck. These veins carry oxygen-depleted blood from the brain, face, and neck, and transport it to the heart. A favoured site for insertion of large bore intravenous lines to administer drugs, for temporary dialysis and also to provide intravenous nutrition.

Intracranial pressure: pressure inside the skull, in brain tissue and in cerebrospinal fluid (CSF) which surrounds the brain

Ischaemic heart disease: narrowing of the arteries that take blood and oxygen to the heart, thereby preventing it from working properly

Mastitis: an inflammation of breast tissue often caused by blocked milk ducts that can result in infection, usually with a bacterium called *Staphylococcus aureus*

Meningococcal disease: a bacterial infection that can be the pre-cursor to septicaemia (blood infection) or meningitis (inflammation of the membranes covering the brain)

Myocardial infarction: see 'heart attack'

Nasogastric tube: a tube that is inserted through the nose, down the back of the throat and into the stomach. Commonly inserted to deflate and empty the stomach prior to airway manoeuvres; to help sick children breathe more effectively; and to supply nutrients to a patient who cannot eat.

Nephron: The functional unit of the kidney comprised of the glomerulus and a series of tubules

Noradrenaline: a medication to improve a patient's blood pressure and cardiac function

Obstructive sleep apnoea: a potentially serious sleep disorder in which breathing repeatedly stops and starts during sleep

Oximeter: a device that measures the amount of oxygen in the blood usually via a finger probe

Petechial rash: tiny spots on the skin caused by bleeding as a result of low platelets in blood and, sometimes, fragile capillaries. Petechial haemorrhages are commonly present in those with meningococcal disease.

Polyphagia: an obsessive desire to eat

Prader-Willi Syndrome: a complex genetic condition, characterized in infancy by weak muscle tone (hypotonia), feeding difficulties, poor growth, and delayed development. In childhood, affected individuals develop an insatiable appetite, which leads to chronic overeating (hyperphagia) and obesity.

Pulmonary hypertension: a type of high blood pressure that affects arteries in the lungs and the right side of the heart. In one form, tiny arteries in the lungs, called pulmonary arterioles, and capillaries become narrowed, blocked or destroyed. This raises the pressure within the lungs' arteries, causing the heart's right ventricle to work harder to pump blood through the lungs, eventually causing the heart muscle to weaken and fail.

Purpura fulmimans: a complication of severe infection that leads to a loss of blood supply to the toes, fingers, and sometimes limbs. Caused by the abnormal formation of clots in the small vessels of the body.

Renal failure: the failure of the kidneys to adequately dispose of waste products

Retroperitoneum: the area of the abdomen that lies behind the kidneys, just below the ribs. Home to the kidneys, pancreas and huge blood vessels and nerves.

Rheumatic disease: a group of conditions that affect the joints and/or connective tissue causing chronic pain

Rheumatic fever: caused by streptococcal infection, an acute fever that causes inflammation and pain in the joints, and long-term damage to heart valves. As a result, bacterial endocarditis—bacterial infection of the heart valves—can occur. This can destroy the heart valves and cause both heart failure and stroke as a result of infected debris flying off the valves and blocking small vessels in the brain.

Shock: a life-threatening condition that results in inadequate flow of blood and oxygen to the tissues of the body. Massive haemorrhage and severe infection are two common causes of shock.

Stridor: a high-pitched noise from the lungs that indicates narrowing of the airway

Tetralogy of Fallot: a congenital malformation of the heart that consists of four structural defects

Thyroxine: a hormone secreted by the thyroid gland, which is primarily responsible for metabolism

Tracheostomy: a procedure where an incision is made into the trachea (windpipe) to insert a breathing tube to restore breathing when there has been a problem with the airway

Tubule: the tiny canals within the kidney that carry the fluid that is initially filtrated by the glomerulus and which eventually ends up as urine

REFERENCES

1 *Saving Lives: Our Healthier Nation* https://www.gov.uk/government/uploads/system/uploads/attachment_data/file/265576/4386.pdf
2 *Solutions to Child Poverty in New Zealand: Evidence for action* http://www.occ.org.nz/assets/Uploads/EAG/Final-report/Final-report-Solutions-to-child-poverty-evidence-for-action.pdf
3 *New Zealand Health Survey: Annual update of key findings 2012/13* http://www.health.govt.nz/publication/new-zealand-health-survey-annual-update-key-findings-2012-13
4   WHO Fact sheet 311
5 Simon Wilson in *Tate Gallery: An Illustrated Companion*, London 1997, p.90